Ordinary Work,

Extraordinary Grace

Ordinary Work,
Extraordinary Grace

My Spiritual Journey in Opus Dei

SCOTT HAHN

DOUBLEDAY *New York London Toronto Sydney Auckland*

PUBLISHED BY DOUBLEDAY

Copyright © 2006 by Scott W. Hahn

All Rights Reserved

Published in the United States by Doubleday, an imprint of
The Doubleday Broadway Publishing Group, a division of
Random House, Inc., New York.
www.doubleday.com

DOUBLEDAY and the portrayal of an anchor with a dolphin
are registered trademarks of Random House, Inc.

Book design by Pei Loi Koay

Cataloging-in-publication data is on file with the Library
of Congress

Nihil Obstat: Reverend Michael F. Hull, STD, Censor Librorum.
Imprimatur: Most Reverend Robert A. Brucato, Auxiliary Bishop
and Vicar General, Archdiocese of New York.

The *Nihil Obstat* and *Imprimatur* are official declarations that
a book or pamphlet is free of doctrinal or moral error. No
implication is contained therein that those who have granted the
Nihil Obstat and the *Imprimatur* agree with the content, opinions,
or statements expressed.

ISBN-13: 978-0-385-519243
ISBN-10: 0-385-519249

PRINTED IN THE UNITED STATES OF AMERICA

10 9 8 7 6 5 4 3 2 1

FIRST EDITION

To Joseph Paul Karl Hahn

Contents

Ordinary Work,

Extraordinary Grace

Chapter 1

A Personal Prelude

How I wish your bearing and conversation were
such that, on seeing or hearing you, people would
say: This man reads the life of Jesus Christ.

—THE WAY, NO. 2

I wasn't yet a Catholic wannabe. I was scared
to be.

A Presbyterian minister, I had taken an
extended sabbatical because I needed the time
to study, pray, and ponder. Over the course
of several years—and much against my deeply
Calvinist and evangelical formation—I had
been reading my way to a Catholic way of
thinking. The more deeply I studied Scripture,
theology, and history—and the more intensely
I prayed—the more inexorably my mind was
drawn to Catholicism.

Yet most of my experience of Catholic
faith came from books. I had spent all of my
post-teenage years in predominantly (and ar-
dently) Protestant environments—first as a
student at a small, private college, then at a
renowned evangelical seminary, and then as

pastor and teacher in some small denominational churches and schools. In all these places, I knew fond fellowship, inspiring leadership, and fervent worship.

On the other hand, my limited exposure to self-identified Catholics—outside of books—had been less than edifying. It came mostly in my teen years, and mostly from kids who were as delinquent as I had been before I accepted Jesus Christ as my Lord and Savior.

Now I was an adult facing an adult crisis. I was a devout Protestant and an ordained minister who found the Catholic arguments more than persuasive—I found them compelling. So I was struggling to choose between all that I loved about my Protestant past and everything I was coming to understand about the Catholic faith. In the evangelicals I knew, I found a deep devotion to Jesus Christ . . . a humble ease in the ways of prayer . . . an astonishing work ethic . . . a zeal for Christianizing culture . . . and a passionate interest in the Scriptures. This last quality was supremely important to me as a preacher of the Word of God and a young biblical theologian. In Catholic doctrine, however, I found an overwhelming coherence, authenticity, and power.

The Bible had brought me to this crisis. At first I had wanted to understand the "covenant theology" of the first Protestant reformers. My research led me to discover that they, especially John Calvin and Martin Luther, were much more "Catholic" in their doctrine than were their modern descendants. Calvin and Luther led me to particular Scriptures—regarding sacraments, church hierarchy and authority, and even Marian doctrine—but just as importantly, they led me to the Church Fathers, those most ancient commentators on Scripture. And it was there, in the writings of the early fathers, that I ran smack up against a church I could only recognize as Catholic. It was liturgical, hierarchical, sacramental. It was Catholic, and yet it held all that I loved about the Reformation tradition too: a deep devotion to Jesus, a spontaneous life of prayer, a zeal to transform the culture, and, of course, a burning love for Scripture.

Still, that Church was real to me only in the dusty books I read. Where, I wanted to know, were the ordinary Catholic believers who lived this way?

Apparently, they were waiting for me in Milwaukee.

Common Ground

I arrived at Marquette University for graduate studies in theology with high hopes but low expectations. But soon I encountered grace upon grace. I met a kind and brilliant pastor who was willing to talk theology with me until the wee hours. He told me of his upbringing in a Polish-American home where family members customarily greeted one another with phrases from the Scriptures. But, I told myself, he was hardly an ordinary Catholic. He held a doctorate from a Roman university; he had served time as a Vatican official; and everyone whispered (rightly, it turns out) that he was on track to become a bishop.

Then I started to meet other Catholics—one a political philosopher, another a dentist—who showed the same qualities. The thing that most impressed me was that they both carried small Bibles in their pockets. At odd moments during the day, I might catch these men sitting in church reading the Scriptures. If I asked them to help me understand a point of doctrine, they would pull out the little book for backup. I thought to myself: *These are men who read the life of Jesus Christ—and read it for all it's worth.*

I mentioned to my priest friend that I had met a couple of guys who always carried the New Testament with them and who really seemed to know it.

He replied, "Oh, they must be Opus Dei."

Opus Dei: I knew enough Latin to know that it meant "the Work of God" or "God's Work." Almost immediately, when I heard Father's words, Opus Dei became for me a beacon—a lighthouse that promised the end of my long voyage, a first glimpse of a land I'd encountered only in books. It's not that the land was too small to be seen; nor was Opus Dei the whole of the land, for the Catholic Church is vaster than anything my denominational experience had prepared me for, and there were then (as there are now) so many other great institutions and movements in the Church. But for many reasons, Opus Dei was someplace where I could begin to feel at home.

What were those reasons?

- First and foremost was its members' apparent devotion to the Bible.
- Second was its warm ecumenism. Opus Dei was the first Catholic institution to welcome non-Catholics to cooperate in its apostolic labors.
- Third was how upright the lives of members were.
- Fourth was how *ordinary* their lives were. They were not theologians—they were dentists, engineers, journalists—but they were talking and living a theology I found attractive.

- Fifth, they espoused a holy ambition—a devout work ethic.
- Sixth, they practiced hospitality and gave their attention generously to my many questions.
- And seventh, they prayed. They made time for intimate prayer every day—true conversation with God. This gave them a serenity I had rarely encountered.

As I grew in my friendships with these men of Opus Dei, I came also to appreciate the rich biblical theology and biblical spirituality at the heart of their vocation. I took these as my own long before God gave me that same vocation—indeed, even before God brought me to the sacraments of the Catholic Church. I recognized immediately that they had tremendous potential for renewing my life, but also the life of Christ's Church, and the life of the world. This book is about Opus Dei's biblical theology and biblical spirituality.

Making Short Work of It

My favorite definition of Opus Dei is the one I found on a prayer card back in the mid-1980s. Opus Dei is "a way of sanctification in daily work and in the fulfillment of the Christian's ordinary duties." It's not just a method of prayer, or an institution in the Church, or a theological school. It's "a way," and that way is wide enough to accommodate everyone whose days are filled with honest work—at home with the kids, in a factory or an office, in the mines, on the farm, or on the battlefield. The way is also wide enough to accommodate free and varied expressions of prayer and theological style and method. God calls some people to commit their lives to this way as the faithful of Opus Dei, but many others take spiritual guidance from Opus Dei and from the books of its founder.

Briefly put: Opus Dei was founded in 1928 by a young Spanish priest, St. Josemaría Escrivá de Balaguer. For years before, he had received presentiments, indications in prayer, that God wanted something from him, but he had no idea what it would be. Then, rather suddenly one October day, as he was sitting down to read over some notes in his journal, *he saw it*. God showed St. Josemaría what He wanted him to do.

The founder rarely spoke about what he "saw" at that moment, but he always used the verb "to see," and he made it clear that he saw Opus Dei in its entirety, as it would unfold through the years. As one Vatican document put it: "It was not a pastoral project which took shape slowly, but rather a call which suddenly burst into the soul of the young priest." What did he see? Perhaps his sketchy private notes give us a glimpse of the vision: "Ordinary Christians. A fermenting mass. Ours is the ordinary, with naturalness. The means: professional work. All saints!" When only three young men showed up for his first formal activities, he gave them benediction with the Blessed Sacrament: "When I blessed those three . . . I saw three hundred, three hundred thousand, thirty million, three billion . . . white, black, yellow, of all the colors, all the combinations that human love can produce."

St. Josemaría saw that Jesus wants everyone to be a saint— everyone, without exception. Our Lord was speaking to the crowd, not to His inner circle, when He said, in the Sermon on the Mount: "Be perfect, just as your heavenly Father is perfect" (Matthew 5:48). *That* is the uncompromising Gospel, the good news that the apostles preached to the nations. St. Paul announced that God "chose us in Him, before the foundation of the world, to be holy and without blemish" (Ephesians 1:4). Moreover, God has made known His "plan" for us, "the mystery of His will." In the fullness of time—which is right now, today—we are "to restore all things in Christ" (Ephesians 1:10).

St. Josemaría taught that all human activity—political life, family life, social life, labor and leisure—should be restored to Christ, offered to God as a pleasing sacrifice, united with the sacrifice of the cross, united with the sacrifice of the Mass. He longed for a day when "in every place in the world there will be Christians with a dedication that is personal and totally free—Christians who will be other Christs."

St. Josemaría saw creation as a great cosmic liturgy, offered to the Father by those "other Christs" in union with Christ the high priest.

Priestly Soul, Lay Mentality

We can make this offering because we are a "royal priesthood, a holy nation" (1 Peter 2:9). We share in Christ's priesthood and kingship because, through baptism, we share in His nature (see 2 Peter 1:4). St. Josemaría urged Christians to have a "truly priestly soul and a fully lay mentality." This is not a contradiction. For, as both priests and kings, we have a vocation that is both sacred and secular. We share in Christ's kingship; we share in His priesthood. So we sanctify the temporal order and offer it to God, restore it "in Christ" because we live in Christ. We restore it, a little bit at a time, beginning with the inch or the yard or the mile over which we've been given dominion. Our workspace, our living space—these are where we exercise our dominion and our priesthood. Our altar is our desktop, our workstation, the row we hoe, the ditch we dig, the diaper we change, the pot we stir, the bed we share with our spouse. All of it is sanctified by our offering hands, which are Christ's own.

This doctrine is a particular emphasis of Opus Dei, but it is the property of the whole Church. The kingship and the priesthood, the rights and the duties, belong not just to a privileged few, not just to the ordained clergy, but to all baptized believers. Our special dignity is that, in baptism, we have become "God's children" (1 John 3:2)—we have joined "the assembly of the firstborn" (Hebrews 12:23). And if we are the firstborn, then we are the heirs (see Galatians 4:7), inheritors of Christ's kingship and the priesthood—the secular (which we are sanctifying) and the sacred. "Everything belongs to you . . .," said St. Paul, "and you to Christ, and Christ to God" (1 Corinthians 3:22–23).

We are God's children. The theological term for this fact is "divine filiation"—and this is the foundation of Opus Dei. It is the source of freedom, confidence, purpose, ardor, and joy for all Christians who live and labor. It is the "open secret" that enables men and women the world over to live out their vocation: to sanctify their work, to sanctify themselves through their work, and to sanctify others through their work.

This is rich fare, I know. Again, we'll spend the rest of the book examining these doctrines in greater detail.

Form Fitting

St. Josemaría spent the rest of his life preaching what God had revealed to him. At first he didn't even give it a name. His spiritual director suggested "Opus Dei," quite by accident, when one day he asked, "How is that work of God coming along?"

Gradually, the organizational details became clear to St. Josemaría, though the Church's canon law could not yet accommodate the institution as God had revealed it. St. Josemaría guided the development of the Work—cautiously, so that it never fell permanently into an inappropriate institutional form, even though it had to pass through a number of temporary, inadequate provisions. In 1965 the Second Vatican Council introduced the idea of a new form, a "personal prelature"—an institution having both lay and clergy members that could carry out specific apostolic tasks. The word *personal* means that the institution's leader, its prelate, has authority not over a territory (as an ordinary bishop does) but over a certain group or sort of persons, wherever those persons may be. In the case of Opus Dei, they are the "faithful" of the prelature—those who are called to make a permanent, personal dedication to this particular "way of sanctification." Whether married or celibate, they make their definitive commitment (which takes the form of a contract) when they make their "oblation," and they renew this commitment annually. At some point, they may recognize the permanence of their vocation more solemnly, by making "the fidelity"—essentially extending the term of the contract to the course of a lifetime.

St. Josemaría recognized the personal prelature as the perfect form for Opus Dei. He did not, however, live to see his family arrive in its home. He died in 1975. In 1982 Pope John Paul II established Opus Dei as the Church's first personal prelature. As I set pen to paper, there are around 85,000 members—again, "faithful" is the Church's preferred term—in the prelature of Opus Dei. The vast majority of them are ordinary laypeople. A small number are priests.

Extra Ordinary

The stories of Opus Dei's founding could give the wrong impression, and perhaps that's why St. Josemaría discussed them so infrequently. The founding of Opus Dei was the occasion of some documented miracles and extraordinary revelations. Yet the emphasis of Opus Dei is decidedly on *ordinary* life, *ordinary* work, and *ordinary* religious experience.

Perhaps the miracles were necessary because of the truly radical nature of God's plan for St. Josemaría. It was a plan that seemed out of step with the times in the early twentieth century, a time when Catholic leaders emphasized the dignity of the clergy almost to the exclusion of the ordinary baptized believer. In Europe, as in the United States, the ordinary, universal, baptismal call to holiness was not an accepted theological opinion. St. Josemaría himself faced accusations of heresy.

But God used those extraordinary first graces—visions, miracles, and private revelations—to blaze a trail, a way, through ordinary life. Sometimes you need to use heavy explosives to build a highway, but rarely to maintain one.

So now we focus on ordinary life. God gives His children dominion over the world (Genesis 1:26) and invites them to enjoy the ordinary goodness of His cosmos, which He has created and redeemed. Moreover, He gives us the remarkable gift of participating directly in that creation and redemption.

To give an example of ordinariness in action: members of Opus Dei take seriously the Church's call to apostolate. But you won't often find them on street corners thumping Bibles or knocking on strangers' doors to give their testimony to Jesus. St. Josemaría taught instead a quiet apostolate of "friendship and confidence"—everyday realities—in which members look for ways to serve others. It might mean inviting a friend to lunch rather than a prayer meeting, or challenging him to racquetball instead of a doctrinal debate.

It's all so very ordinary. Yet this doctrine itself has the power to shock people. The modern world—and even some folks in the Church—have turned so topsy-turvy that an emphasis on the ordinary is, for them, a truly extraordinary thing!

Going on Vocation

By now it is probably superfluous to say that, eventually, this Calvinist became a Catholic—and that my first contacts with Opus Dei were important milestones on my way to the Catholic Church. Maybe you've also guessed that I received a vocation to Opus Dei as well.

In daring to write this book, I do not wish to hold myself up as a model or paragon of Opus Dei. Nor is this book in any sense an official statement of the Work (as Opus Dei is sometimes called colloquially), its aims, and its principles. Still less is it a critical analysis of Opus Dei's organizational structure or status in canon law. All those books have already been written, and written very well.

This book is, rather, my own reflection on the vocation I share with so many others—men and women who excel me in wisdom, in every virtue, and in the everyday living of Opus Dei. It is also a public expression of gratitude to God for a grace I do not deserve—a grace that I hope many people will come to share, as much as God wills them to share it.

Since I am, by trade and by training, a biblical theologian, this book applies the tools of my peculiar (and entirely sancti-fiable) profession to the core ideas of Opus Dei.

Chapter 2

The Secret of Opus Dei

What a wonderful thing it is to be a child! When
a man asks a favor, his request must be backed by
a list of his qualifications. When it is a child who
asks—since children haven't any qualifications—
it's enough for him to say: I'm a son of So-and-so.
Ah, Lord—say it to Him with all your heart!—I
am a son of God!

—THE WAY, NO. 892

Sometimes young preachers get carried away
with enthusiasm for their subject. They so im-
merse themselves in study that the current
topic, whatever it may be, seems the interpre-
tive key to every other topic, theme, crux, and
conundrum.

Such must have been the case for one
young priest of Opus Dei. He was newly ordained and stationed in Rome, close to the his-
toric and administrative heart of the Catholic
Church, and especially close to Monsignor
Escrivá, who was then still living and very
much involved in the day-to-day life of the
Work.

What a joy, then, when the young priest was called upon to deliver a meditation at the Opus Dei center where the founder lived and worked. The assigned subject was "humility."

Opus Dei priests, like all members, are exhorted to do their work with the utmost professional excellence, since they are offering that work to God. Thus, a preacher should prepare his sermons with due diligence, researching what the saints and scholars have to say about the topic at hand. A member of any other institution in the Church will also consult the relevant works of his institution's founder. No problem there: Monsignor Escrivá had written plenty of material about humility.

Thus, we can be fairly certain that our young priest had prepared himself very well to talk about humility. No doubt, he was even humbled before the immensity of his topic, and in his mind and in his preaching he projected it larger than life into the dimly lit chapel.

At a certain point in his meditation, he said with conviction: "The spiritual foundation of Opus Dei is humility." And perhaps he paused to let the point sink in.

For into that small opening came a sudden, firm, and fatherly voice from the back of the chapel: "No, it's not!"

From out of the shadows came St. Josemaría, taking decisive steps toward the place where the young man was preaching. The old saint, addressing the young man as "my son," motioned him up from his chair.

We must be careful not to misunderstand this moment. St. Josemaría held courtesy in high regard. He was not a man who went about interrupting people to correct them whenever they uttered a slight imprecision. But neither did he consider it discourteous to shout "Fire!" in a burning building. To misrepresent the spirit of Opus Dei—even out of youthful exuberance—was that kind of moment. In a center of Opus Dei, it called for emergency measures.

So he himself finished the meditation, revealing to his listeners—who were now keenly attentive—the true spiritual foundation of Opus Dei.

It is, he said, *divine filiation*.

Coming to Terms

Divine filiation. What should we make of this curious, Latinate, technical term from theology? According to St. Josemaría, we should make it the center of our lives.

The meaning is simple and biblical: *we are God's children now* (1 John 3:2). It is simple and familiar, but perhaps too familiar. The "fatherhood of God and the brotherhood of man" is, by now, a worn coin, a cultural cliché—even for many non-Christians. The doctrine, once central to the preaching of the Gospel, has been, perhaps, too well assimilated. It has lost the shock value it had for Christianity's first generation. When St. John spoke about divine filiation, even after many decades of preaching, he still could not hide his astonishment: "See what love the Father has given us, that we should be called children of God; and so we are!" (1 John 3:1).

And so we are! Think, for a moment, about the marvels of human conception and birth that have been recorded on film, thanks to nano-photography. Considering all the natural obstacles, it seems remarkable that any sperm should ever fertilize any egg, and that any egg should ever succeed in implantation, and that any embryo should ever develop into a fetus—and that any child should endure, *in utero,* to be born. Even hardened secularists find themselves slackjawed when they consider mere *human filiation.* The television series *Nova,* aired in the United States by the Public Broadcasting Service, felt compelled to title its baby-making documentary "The *Miracle* of Birth."

Human filiation is itself a wonder. Yet it pales in comparison with the supernatural birth, the divine filiation that Christians receive in baptism. There we become identified with Christ, united with Christ, empowered to live His life—raised to share the life of the eternal Son of God in the Blessed Trinity. In baptism, then, we become, like Jesus, children of almighty and eternal God—children of a Father who can give us all we need, a Father who is perfect, all-knowing, and omnipresent, a Father who keeps all His promises and does not make mistakes.

Divine filiation is the reason we are baptized. It is the very substance of heaven. It is what the New Testament means when it speaks of "salvation," "sanctification," and "justification." St. Josemaría made so bold as to call the process "divinization" and "deification"—mere human beings come to share in the divine nature; they become godlike. They live as God's children in the eternal divine family, the Trinity.

Through baptism, we become God's children, for we live in Christ. We are, in the cherished phrase of the Church Fathers, "sons in the Son." Throughout the long Farewell Discourse of St. John's gospel, Jesus describes His own communion with the Father and His simultaneous communion with believers: "I am in My Father and you are in Me and I in you" (John 14:20).

Christ is the *only* begotten Son of God. So our sonship is not the same as His, but it is a share in His. We are not God. But Jesus Himself described our sonship by saying, "You are gods" (John 10:34; see also Psalms 82:6). His sonship is uncreated and eternal. Ours is a grace; it is created; it is adoptive. But it is real. Through baptism, we are more truly His children than we are children of our earthly moms and dads. Through baptism, we are more truly at home in heaven than in the place where we grew up. St. Maximus Confessor put it this way: we "become completely whatever God is, save at the level of being," and we receive for ourselves "the whole of God Himself," in all His infinity, in all His eternity. As St. John of Damascus put it: we become by grace what God is by nature.

This seems paradoxical: the finite contains the infinite. But it is God Himself who made this possible, by assuming human flesh in Jesus Christ. In doing so, He humanized His divinity, but He also divinized humanity, and thus He sanctified—made holy—everything that fills up a human life: friendship, meals, family, travel, study, and work.

A Streetcar Named Divine

I don't want to give the impression that this is all theoretical and wholly inexpressible apart from words ending in *-ization*. I'm a theologian and a professor, and we do tend to talk about things that way. St. Josemaría was a teacher himself, with two earned doctorates, but he did not find divine filiation at the end of a syllogism, and only rarely did he speak of it in the terms of academic theology. For him it began with a much more immediate and visceral experience.

The year was 1931, three years since the founding vision, yet he had little to show for his prayer and efforts. He was suffering too, because of the turmoil in Spain's society—the conditions that would eventually lead to the bloody Spanish Civil War. Poverty was widespread, morals were plummeting, and anti-Catholic violence was on the rise. The storm center, of course, was the capital, Madrid, where he was living.

On the morning of October 16, after saying Mass, he tried to pray "in the quiet of my church," but he found it impossible. He went out and bought a newspaper before boarding a streetcar. Settling into his seat, he started reading the news of the day when suddenly and very intensely he "felt the action of the Lord." He later explained that God "was making spring forth in my heart and on my lips, with the force of something imperatively necessary, this tender invocation, *Abba! Pater!*"

Though he had been unable to pray in the quiet sanctuary, suddenly—in the noisy street, on a crowded streetcar—he was awash in prayer. And his prayer was simply "Father!" Or, more precisely, "Daddy!" In Aramaic, the language Jesus spoke, *Abba* is the intimate, colloquial form of address that small children would use with their father. Jesus used it in prayer, as did St. Paul. *Pater* is the Latin word for "Father," which recurs so often in the Mass.

But these were not mere words. That very day, in his journal, St. Josemaría recorded the experience as "a prayer of copious and ardent feelings of affection." The prayer on his lips, though, was irrepressible. He got off the streetcar and wandered the busy streets, but still could not stop invoking his heavenly Father: *Abba! Pater! Abba! Pater! Abba! Pater!* Nor could he mark the time; it lasted "maybe an hour, maybe two." The as-

tonished passersby "must have thought I was crazy," he later recalled. Not till that morning, that streetcar ride, had he recognized the meaning of God's fatherhood, for his life, for the
world, and for the Work that was aborning. He would refer to
the experience as his "first prayer as a son of God." He saw immediately, moreover, the significance of the event for the spirituality of Opus Dei.

God had kept him from praying in the quiet church but
gave him an abundant gift of prayer in the middle of the ordinary, workaday world. From that moment on, he never wa-
vered in his conviction: "Divine filiation," he would often say, "is
the basis of the spirit of Opus Dei."

What are the consequences? "By living their divine filiation, my children would find themselves filled with joy and
peace, protected by an impregnable wall; and would know how
to be apostles of this joy, and how to communicate their peace,
even in the face of their own or another's suffering. Just because of that: because we are convinced that God is our Father."

Like Father, Like Son

To know God as Father is to know the God of Christians, the
God of Jesus Christ. For God's fatherhood is a uniquely Christian idea. Only Christians identify "Father" as God's proper
name. Other religions say that God is *like* a father, because creation is, in some ways, *like* human reproduction, or because divine providence is, in some ways, *like* the care of earthly
providers. But in non-Christian religions divine fatherhood is
ultimately metaphorical. God acts in a fatherly way only in relation to other beings—the world, the human race, or a chosen

people. God is fatherly only once he has created something or someone to care for. Thus, divine fatherhood, in the non-Christian sense, is dependent upon other beings. It is related to God's action in time, but it is not of His essence.

For Muslims, to speak of God as "father" is simply blasphemy, a violation of God's transcendence and simplicity. For Jews, God *acts* as father to His chosen people, but his fatherhood does not precede their creation and election.

Only Christians dare to say that God is "Father" from all eternity—before time, before creation. He is "Father" in Himself, because He eternally fathers the Son within the Blessed Trinity.

So, for Christians, God's fatherhood is of His essence. "Father" is who He is. Divine fatherhood, then, is *not* metaphorical; it is metaphysical. It would be more accurate to say that human fatherhood is metaphorical, a temporal sign of an eternal reality. God's fatherhood is true fatherhood in the truest sense.

God is the eternal Father of Jesus Christ. And God is Father of those who live in Jesus Christ, through baptism.

The *Gospel Truth*

This is hardly a novelty. It is, rather, a recovery of something classic in Christianity. St. Josemaría said that it is "as old as the Gospel but, like the Gospel, ever new."

The Old Testament references to God's fatherhood are few and, by themselves, ambiguous. Indeed, the first four chapters of the *New* Testament do not mention God's fatherhood at all. Then suddenly, when Jesus begins His preaching—when He

delivers His defining statement, the Sermon on the Mount—
the idea dominates. In that one sermon, God is called Father
seventeen times—far more than in the entire Old Testament.
At the climax of the sermon, Jesus teaches the crowd to pray
to God as "Our Father"—a stunning and revolutionary new
way of prayer.

Our divine filiation is the centerpiece of the Gospel as
Jesus preached it. It is the very meaning of the salvation He
won for us. For He did not merely save us *from* our sins; He
saved us *for* sonship. The *Catechism of the Catholic Church* puts it
succinctly: "By His death, Christ liberates us from sin; by His
Resurrection, He opens for us the way to a new life. This new
life is above all justification that reinstates us in God's grace, 'so
that as Christ was raised from the dead by the glory of the Father, we too might walk in newness of life.' Justification con-
sists in both victory over the death caused by sin and a new
participation in grace. It brings about filial adoption so that
men become Christ's brethren."

Divine sonship was the gift that God intended for Adam
and Eve at the beginning of creation. God made the primal
couple "in His own image" and "likeness" (Genesis 1:26–27; see
also Genesis 5:1). The only other time the Bible uses this phrase
is to describe human fatherhood, when Adam begot Seth (Genesis 5:3). Indeed, at the moment of man's creation, God
"breathed into his nostrils the breath of life; and man became a
living being" (Genesis 2:7). This was not mere biological life,
not mere animal respiration, but divine life. God breathed His
breath—his *ruah,* His Spirit—into Adam, and not into any
other animal. In the beginning, God empowered man and
woman to share His life, to live in intimacy with Him. Adam

and Eve, however, chose to "be like God" (Genesis 3:5), not on His terms, but on their own. Their original sin, then, was a rejection of divine filiation. And God respected their choice.

Jesus's salvation consisted in restoring humanity's original dignity, fulfilling God's original intention for creation. "Beloved, we are God's children now." Nothing was more important to the first Christians—or to that man on a streetcar in Madrid in 1931. St. Paul told the Galatians: "And because you are sons, God has sent the Spirit of his Son into our hearts, crying, 'Abba! Father!' " (Galatians 4:6).

A Forgotten Doctrine?

This is classic Christianity. Yet no Christian historian can deny that, in recent centuries, divine filiation has been reshuffled in the deck of doctrine. The language of "divinization" and "deification"—the common coin of the Church Fathers—fell into such disuse that Cardinal Christoph Schönborn, in 1988, wrote an essay defending the very idea. He cites many historical reasons why Christians had forgotten their filiation. I would like to add one more to his list, a reason that would loom large for me as I first, tentatively, approached the Catholic faith.

I believe that the idea of divine filiation got lost amid all the post-Reformation debate over the relationship of faith, works, and justification. For four centuries, Catholic and Protestant theologians alike had focused so narrowly on these controversies that they obscured the central fact of Christian life. The reformers were challenging certain dogmas of the Church, and so the Church had to respond by turning its own attention to those disputed dogmas. It was the running argument that reshuffled the doctrinal deck. Post-Reformation Catholic writers felt compelled to emphasize precisely the points that Protestants denied. All this was necessary, in a remedial way. But its lingering effect was to produce a theology that was somewhat misshapen and off-center.

What captivated me about the Protestant reformers was their emphasis on the "covenant"—a dominant reality throughout the Bible, which is itself divided into the "Old Covenant" and the "New Covenant." John Calvin especially saw covenant as the key to understanding our justification, sanctification, and salvation. For Calvin, however, "covenant" meant roughly the same thing as "contract," and so his spiritual progeny tended to speak of Christian religion in legal terms, of rights and duties and terms of exchange.

Modern covenant research, however, showed me something entirely different. An ancient covenant was more than a contract. It was the means by which two unrelated parties struck a *family* bond. They became siblings, spouses, or parent and child. Marriage was a covenant; adoption was a covenant.

With His covenant, then, God was not just laying down a law. He was raising up a family. The inevitable consequence of covenant is divine filiation.

Imagine my joy when, as a Protestant, I first encountered St. Josemaría's teaching. Here was a man who spoke of redemption predominantly in familial and familiar terms: God as father, the Church as family, Mary as mother of all believers, the human race as brothers and sisters, and all the baptized, of course, as God's children. "The work of our Redemption has been accomplished. We are now children of God, because Jesus has died for us and His death has ransomed us. *Empti enim estis pretio magno!* (1 Corinthians 6:20), you and I have been bought at a great price."

For me, Opus Dei represented a reintegration of Christian experience, a recovery of the ancient unity that had somehow gotten lost amid the shouting matches of recent history. I did not know anyone in the Protestant world who spoke with the Gospel freshness I encountered in the lay and clergy members of Opus Dei.

When I read the words that he preached, he seemed to be preaching to me. "Isn't it true," St. Josemaría once said, "that you have seen the need to become a soul of prayer, to reach an intimacy with God that leads to divinization? Such is the Christian faith as always understood by souls of prayer." And as if to prove the "always" part, he goes on to quote St. Clement of Alexandria, who wrote around the year 203 A.D.: "A man becomes God, because he loves whatever God loves."

Chapter 3

The Catholic Work Ethic

That work—humble, monotonous, small—is
prayer expressed in action that prepares you to
receive the grace of the other work—great and
wide and deep—of which you dream.

THE WAY, NO. 825

Sometimes advertisements give us the most
accurate—and painful—insights into popular
religion. I once saw a magazine ad that proclaimed: "If the original sin had been sloth,
we'd still be in paradise."

The copywriter meant it as a joke, of
course. But he knew that he was tapping into
something powerful: the common notion that
the ideal life would provide uninterrupted idle
time and that work is for vacation in much the
same way that life is for heaven. In the words
of the popular song, "Everybody's working for
the weekend."

The flip side of this notion is more insidi-
ous, and it keeps many people laboring under
an illusion. It is the belief that work is a punishment for sin. Advocates of this theory usually

invoke God's condemnation of Adam after he had sinned: "Cursed is the ground because of you! In toil you shall eat of it all the days of your life; thorns and thistles it shall bring forth to you; and you shall eat the plants of the field. In the sweat of your face you shall eat bread till you return to the ground" (Genesis 3:17–19).

The passage does seem to give a bleak forecast for the long-term conditions of human work. And it does portray tiresome toil as a punishment for sin. The punishment, however, is not the work itself but the harsh conditions of work that make it tedious, frustrating, and arduous.

Work itself was one of God's original blessings. St. Josemaría delighted in pointing out that, "from the beginning of creation man has had to work . . . before sin entered the world, and in its wake death, punishment, and misery (cf. Romans 5:12). God made Adam from the clay of the earth, and created for him and his descendants this beautiful world we live in, *ut operaretur et custodiret illum* (Genesis 2:15), so that we might cultivate it and look after it."

God made Adam because "there was no man to till the ground" (Genesis 2:5). There was a job opening, a job description, and a job to do. God Himself created the perfect candidate for the position. And remember, all this took place at a time when the world knew no sin or unhappiness. God made man and woman for work, and so they could not—and we cannot—find fulfillment apart from work.

Yet even more than He made man and woman for the sake of work, He made work for the sake of man and woman—because only through work could they become truly godlike. It's not that they earn the grace of divinization by the strength of their labors. For grace is a gift and cannot be earned. Rather, work itself is a gift that makes men and women ever more like God.

Indeed, Genesis depicts God Himself *at work* as He creates the world: "And on the seventh day God finished His work . . . and He rested . . . from all His work which He had done" (Genesis 2:2). Thus, work itself is something divine, something God Himself does. So it is a godly and godlike activity for those who are made in God's image and likeness. When human beings work, they imitate their creator; they share His life. For He made the earth out of nothing, but He willed that a creature should till and keep it. He willed that His earthly children should keep the family grounds and thus grow to live more perfectly in the image of their heavenly Father. He willed that work itself should be a cooperative act of creation, a co-creation, by both the Father and His heirs.

Terms and Conditions

God gave humanity work when He gave Adam life, in a time of pristine innocence. Genesis tells the story with the utmost economy, making every word count. We should take a moment and examine the terms of the work God gave us.

God's command for Adam "to till [the garden] and keep it" employs two Hebrew verbs, *'abodah* and *shamar*. Both words are rich, and both are capable of dual meanings. They appear together elsewhere in the Bible—and whenever they do they are describing the ministerial duties of the Levites, ancient Israel's priestly tribe (see Numbers 3:7–8, 8:26, 18:5–6). The verb *'abodah,* often translated as "serve," has in Hebrew a dual meaning: it can denote either manual labor or priestly ministry (as in a "worship service"), or it can suggest both meanings. The verb *shamar* means "to keep" or "to guard," and it describes the Levites' protection of the holy place, the tabernacle, which they guarded and kept from defilement.

Many Scripture scholars believe that the author of the Book of Genesis intended to suggest all of this in the story of Adam's creation. God made Adam to work, and God made him to be a priest in the cosmic temple. These were not separate activities. In the beginning, Adam enjoyed a unity of life; his work was ordered to worship and was itself an act of worship. The very division of time reflected this ordering principle. God Himself worked six days so that He might hallow the seventh day, making it holy. God built the Sabbath rhythm into the fabric of creation.

We work so that we might worship more perfectly. We worship while we work. When the first Christians cast about for a word to describe their worship, they chose *leitourgia,* a word that, like the Hebrew *'abodah,* could indicate ritual worship but could also mean "public work," as in the labor of street sweepers or the men who lit the streetlamps at night. The meaning is evident to those who know the biblical languages, whether or not they are steeped in the Catholic liturgical tradition. The British Protestant biblical scholar C. F. D. Moule put the matter well:

> But the striking way in which what we might describe
> as "secular" words such as *leitourgein* (to render civic
> service) are applied also to "divine service" provides
> a very salutary reminder that worship, for a truly

religious person, is the be all and end all of work; and
that if worship and work are distinguished, that is only
because of the frailty of human nature which cannot
do more than one thing at a time. The necessary
alternation between lifting up holy hands in prayer and
swinging an axe in strong, dedicated hands for the
glory of God is the human makeshift for that single,
simultaneous, divine life in which work is worship and
worship is the highest possible activity. And the single
word "liturgy" in the New Testament, like 'abodah,
"work" or "service," in the Old Testament, covers both.

Once again, we see that work is an earthly image of God's activity, and thus the worker is an image (and likeness) of God.
Since God is eternal, His activity is simple and unified. Since
we live in time, our activity is differentiated—and, too often,
diffuse. But by our sharing in God's life, our own lives begin to
acquire a simplicity, a unity of work and worship.

Yet this simplicity often eludes modern Christians, who
tend to put work and prayer in separate, airtight compart-
ments. St. Josemaría often warned people of "the temptation . . . to lead a kind of double life: on the one hand, an
inner life, a life related to God; and on the other, as something
separate and distinct, their professional, social and family lives,
made up of small earthly realities." For this attitude he reserved
strong words: "No, my children! We cannot lead a double
life. . . . There is only one life, made of flesh and spirit. And it
is that life which has to become, in both body and soul, holy
and filled with God: we discover the invisible God in the most
visible and material things."

St. Josemaría went on to speak of this integrated life as a restoration of that opening scene of Genesis: "That is why I tell you that our age needs to give back to matter and to the apparently trivial events of life their noble, original meaning. It needs to place them at the service of the Kingdom of God."

The Word at Work

In this work of restoration, Jesus Christ was, of course, the first on the job. Quite simply, He worked. His contemporaries knew Him to be a skilled laborer, in Greek a *tekton,* a craftsman. Tradition relates that His particular craft was carpentry. Jesus's neighbors marveled that an ordinary laborer could study the Scriptures, grow wise, and teach with authority, as this man did. "Isn't this the carpenter?" they asked (Mark 6:3). Elsewhere they mention that He was also the son of a craftsman (Matthew 13:55).

But it was of His *heavenly* Father that He said: "My Father is working still, and I am working" (John 5:17). Jesus was always at work, and His work was one with His divine life and divine worship. He was always creating, redeeming, and sanctifying the world, and He was always united with His Father in the love of the Holy Spirit. All of the discrete, earthly actions of His life were earthly manifestations of that one, simple, eternal life, that serene yet dynamic heavenly activity. Thus, *everything* He did was redemptive—not just His suffering and death on the cross. His hours spent in the carpentry shop had a redeeming value, an atoning efficacy. He offered His work to God, and all these works worked to save the world.

As a carpenter and head of a household, Jesus lived the

common priesthood that God had intended for Adam—and for all of us on earth. In this, as in everything, He is our model. But He is more than that. In baptism and Holy Communion, He is united with us. So we not only imitate Him; we participate in His life. He works in us, and we work in Him. We offer our work, as a priestly offering, a redemptive sacrifice, for the sake of our family members, neighbors, coworkers, and friends. And with Christ, we create the world anew, with our labors and our prayers.

This isn't just pie in the sky. It's the pie on the table too—for the mother who baked it and offered it to God. It's the pie chart on the slides—for the broker preparing a presentation. It's the *pi* in the equation—for the high school geometry teacher preparing her lesson plans.

All of this, when done well and offered to God, advances the cause of God's creation and wins the redemption of the world. It really works.

On Earth as It Is in Heaven

It's fair to ask: If Jesus restored the original plan for work, why do our labors today still bear the marks of Adam's sin? Why must our work be fraught with sweat, frustration, tedium, and failure? Why must my back ache at the end of each workday when the factory whistle blows?

We should note that Jesus did not exempt His own earthly life from suffering. His labors were difficult, as ours are. And He suffered misunderstanding, false accusation, the envy of other teachers, and—on Calvary—apparent failure.

It is true to say, as Protestant evangelicals do, that Jesus paid a debt He did not owe because we owed a debt we could not pay. But Christ was not merely our substitute. If He had been, we might rightly ask why we still have to bear the punishment for Adam's sin: why must our work still be arduous? As our substitute, Christ should have eliminated the need for our suffering, right?

Wrong. Christ was not our substitute but our representative, and since His saving passion was representative, it doesn't exempt us from suffering but rather endows our suffering with divine power and redemptive value. St. Paul said: "Now I rejoice in my sufferings for your sake, and in my flesh I complete what is lacking in Christ's afflictions for the sake of His body, that is, the Church" (Colossians 1:24). What can be lacking in Christ's perfect sufferings? Only what He wills to be lacking, because He wants us to be His co-redeemers, His co-workers.

Jesus did not eradicate suffering, but He did enable us to suffer as He did. He endowed our suffering with divine power and redemptive value. And for that reason, St. Paul could actually "rejoice" in his suffering, for Christ's sake! This is the deep, scriptural source of St. Josemaría's spirit of joyful mortification, which is so often misunderstood: "Let us bless pain," he wrote. "Love pain. Sanctify pain. . . . Glorify pain!" He is not saying anything so inane as "pain is good," but rather that, through pain, we can accomplish great good—and more, God can cultivate great holiness—in our lives. Through pain we can grow more like Jesus Christ in His suffering.

So our work is hard, but you really can't beat the benefits, because they're dispensed by almighty God. And they're benefits we can apply not just to our immediate family but to all the people in our lives and all the people of the world, for the living and for the dead, for the eternal rest of our ancestors and for the perseverance of our descendants in the Christian faith. And we can live in joyful hope that all those people will come to pray and offer their work for us as well. That's some benefits package. The creed calls it the "communion of saints."

Blessed by Success?

When I was a Presbyterian minister, I was justly proud of what social scientists called the "Protestant work ethic." The sociologist Max Weber coined the phrase to describe a certain attitude he noticed in Calvinists. They worked hard, and they consistently tried to do their professional best. It's not that they thought they could earn a ticket to heaven. Rather, they believed that everyone on earth was predestined to heaven or hell, and that earthly success could be a providential sign of God's favor, of election, of a heavenly destiny. Weber was at least partially right when he tagged this ethic as the power behind the capitalist dynamo.

But the Protestant work ethic was not a Christian dogma. It was a sociological phenomenon (though, indeed, a mighty one). What we have seen in the Book of Genesis goes far deeper than any cultural trends and is not a work ethic, but something fuller and more robust. It is a true "theology of work," a metaphysics of work. It is not just some believers' collective response to the creed, but a truth built into the fabric of creation.

Moreover, it does not depend upon worldly success. As

Blessed Mother Teresa often said: God doesn't ask us to be successful, just faithful.

Faithfulness means that we'll always try to do our best. But it doesn't guarantee we'll get a pay raise, or be promoted, or win the election. We might still get docked, or downsized, or injured on the job. Still, the theology of work is a more powerful motivator than any mere work ethic: it makes the *audacious* claim that the work we do can get us to heaven—and redeem many other souls too—not because it's our work but because it's God's work, *opus Dei*. Whether the world counts us a success or failure is secondary; we want such success only to glorify God. What is primary is that we work with God's hands, with the mind of Christ (1 Corinthians 2:16). St. Teresa of Avila spoke of the awesome dignity that Christ has given us as His coworkers:

> Christ has no body now but yours,
> No hands, no feet on earth but yours,
> Yours are the eyes with which He looks
> Compassion on this world,
> Yours are the feet with which He walks to do good,
> Yours are the hands, with which He blesses all the world.

Jesus was faithful to the end, and that is precisely what constituted His success. He accomplished the will of His Father, and He saved the world with the blood that marked His "defeat." He continues to work the marvels of redemption through His brothers and sisters, in our successes and in our failures, in all the work we offer with Him to God our Father.

Needless to say, we should always do the best we can,

because nothing less than our best is worthy to be placed on the altar for God. Read the Old Testament prophets and learn what happened when the Temple priests got lazy or greedy and started offering lame and blemished animals to God. They wanted to keep the best for themselves. And we can do the same with our time, our attention, and our efforts. Such selfishness turned out badly for Israel, and it can turn out badly for us too. If our work is worship, it had better be good!

One last word: Jesus taught us, by word and example, to work hard, but not to idolize work or the money we can earn by working hard. When God made the world, He divided time in such a way that we should never forget the reason we're working. He worked six days in order to hallow the seventh. We too must keep holy the Lord's day. Our six days of work are ordered to one of purer worship.

God made us for this Sabbath rest, and our bodies and our work show forth His intelligent design. It is human to long for the Sabbath rest. It is human to need the Sabbath. The U.S. military found this out the hard way back in the 1940s. In order to make ambitious quotas, the government asked its munitions plants to extend the workweek to seven days, round the clock. Most plants complied, but some didn't. Interestingly enough, the only plants that made their quotas were the plants that closed on Sundays. Their workers were better rested and thus more efficient, and they suffered fewer on-the-job injuries. As Jesus pointed out, the Sabbath was made for man (Mark 2:27). It fulfills a need of body, mind, and spirit. In that sense, man was made for the Sabbath too.

Some years after I became a Catholic, and some years after I joined Opus Dei, I was pleased to attend the Church's Mass to mark the memorial of the newly declared Blessed Josemaría Escrivá. I thrilled to hear the first reading the Church had chosen for the Mass. It was from the Book of Genesis: "The Lord God took the man and put him in the garden of Eden to till it and keep it" (Genesis 2:15).

Chapter 4

The Work and the Church

What joy to be able to say with all the fervor
of my soul: I love my Mother the holy Church!

—THE WAY, NO. 518

Whenever filmmakers or newspaper editors want to signify the Catholic Church, they reach for an image that will be immediately recognizable to everyone: a bank of stained-glass windows refracting brilliant sunbeams in an explosion of color . . . the spires of a Gothic church or the dome of a basilica . . . a bishop fully vested, with a miter on his head and a crozier in his hand.

For millions of people, those images represent the mission, purpose, and personality of the Church.

But the Church, in its most classic writings, expressed its self-understanding in very different ways: a ship, a vineyard, a fisherman's net, a threshing floor, the transactions of brokers and investors—and most often of all, a household, a family home.

All popular perceptions aside, this is surely

the more accurate set of symbols. The kingdom of God extends through all creation, and on earth we call that kingdom the Church. Yet no earthly kingdom is confined to its palace, and the kingdom of God is not limited to the Church's sanctuaries.

This is a truth, said St. Josemaría, "as old as the gospel and, like the gospel, new," ever new. The Gospel tells us that the Church is the kingdom of God. The Gospel tells us that the Church is the Body of Christ, made up of many members. And none of these doctrines permit us to reduce the Church to its ceremonies and its distinctive architecture.

Most of the members of the Church spend most of their time not in church but at work and at home. Those are the places where they express their Christian faith, where they offer their Christian witness, where they live their Christian lives. It is not for an hour, or even seven hours, of church attendance per week that we have our identity. Nor is our "religious experience" limited to the times we spend at devotions. Our identification with Christ is a permanent thing; our communion with Christ is as constant as the state of grace in our souls. You and I are the Church; that is our identity, and we are Church not only when we are *at* church but always and everywhere.

What's So Special?

If that idea is simply the Gospel truth, classic Christianity, then it's fair to ask why it is so important to our discussion of the distinctive spirit of Opus Dei. The answer is, in part, because "ordinary work" is a particular emphasis in Opus Dei. Consider an analogy with other spiritualities. Every Christian is called to cultivate the virtue of poverty, but God calls a few to renounce all possessions as a special witness. In a similar way, God wants all of us to be chaste and pure, reserving sexual activity as a holy expression of married love, but He calls some people to lead lives of celibacy, renouncing even married love for the sake of the kingdom. As for holiness in ordinary work, one theologian put it well: it makes sense, he said, that there should be "people who set an example and dedicate themselves to that mission."

In the words of St. Josemaría, Opus Dei bears witness that "the Church is present wherever there is a Christian who strives to live in the name of Christ." The founder disagreed strongly with Christians who said that the Church needed to "penetrate" the professions. Penetration was unnecessary, he explained, because the Church was already there—in Catholics who were busy at their work. He told an interviewer: "I hope the time will come when the phrase 'the Catholics are penetrating all sectors of society' will go out of circulation because everyone will have realized that it is a clerical expression. . . . [They] have no need to 'penetrate' the temporal sector for the simple reason that they are ordinary citizens, the same as their fellow citizens, and so they are there already."

To paraphrase the comic strip *Pogo:* wherever you go, there you are—and there is the Catholic Church. No Catholic needs marching orders from the Vatican in order to carry out his daily work. Humankind got the command with its DNA at the moment of creation, and the mandate was renewed in the imitable life of our hardworking Messiah and His apostles. St. Paul knew that his own labor as a tentmaker confirmed the content of his preaching and bolstered his credibility as a

Christian; he urged his hearers to take heed and do honest work themselves.

A Little Bit Goes a Long Way

Opus Dei, then, holds nothing as its own, but rather emphasizes certain things that are the common property of the Church and of Christians: ordinary work, for example, and a passionate love for the world.

When asked in 1958—years before Opus Dei would find its definitive institutional form—to describe the Work, St. Josemaría said simply: "Opus Dei is a little bit of the Church."

In many ways, Opus Dei is *like* a particular church. At a quick glance, it looks like one. It has priests, lay members, and a prelate who guides its spiritual formation. But it is *not* a church within the Church, because its members owe obedience to their local bishop and to the pope, just as all other Catholic faithful do. Opus Dei's authority extends only to the personal spiritual formation of its members.

Still, the similarity is instructive. The theologian Pedro Rodríguez holds that Opus Dei's organizational structure reflects the "primal" or "aboriginal" makeup of the Church: "The structure of the Church . . . is this: priestly ministers, by dedication to their ministry, serve the brethren ('the faithful'), so as to enable the latter, exercising their existential priesthood to serve God and the world."

This view of hierarchy harkens back to the origins of the word in the era of the Church Fathers. In perhaps the fifth century, Dionysius the Areopagite coined the Greek term *hierarchia,* a compound word meaning "sacred rule." When he and

later Fathers spoke of hierarchy, they meant, not a pecking order, but an order of service. This was true in heaven as on
earth. Among the angels, the higher choirs bore the responsibility of serving the lower ones. On earth, the bishops must
place themselves at the service of the clergy, and the clergy in
turn must serve the faithful. At the summit of this pyramid of
service, the pope refers to himself as "the servant of the servants of God."

Thus, the founder of Opus Dei, though he was a priest, did
not seek to gather power to the clergy. In fact, he wanted the
Catholic laity to discover their own dignity and assume the responsibilities that came with baptism. In 1932 he wrote: "The
prejudice that ordinary members of the faithful must limit
themselves to assisting the clergy in ecclesiastical apostolates
has to be rejected. There is no reason why the secular apostolate should always be a mere participation in the apostolate of
the hierarchy. Lay people, too, have a duty to do apostolate: not
because they receive a canonical mission, but because they are
a part of the Church. Their mission . . . is fulfilled in their profession, their job, their family, and among their colleagues and
friends."

Clerical Errors

St. Josemaría wryly described his approach as "a healthy anticlericalism"—which he differentiated from the "evil anticlericalism" that led to the persecution of priests in his native Spain
during the 1930s. In Opus Dei he encouraged the close cooperation of priests and laity as equal "faithful" of the Church,
with distinct but complementary roles in the priestly People of

God. This idea seemed revolutionary in a time when the clergy were viewed as the Church's aristocracy and ruling class, but it is actually not a new idea. Rather, it is another recovery of something classic in Christianity. The journalist John L. Allen noted: "The idea of priests and laity, men and women, all part of one organic whole, sharing the same vocation and carrying out the same apostolic tasks, has not been part of the Catholic tradition, at least since the early centuries."

Allen is right. We have to reach back to the *very* early centuries. The emperor Constantine's decision, in 313 A.D., to "tolerate" Christianity brought an end to centuries of on-again, off-again persecution and bestowed many benefits upon the Church. In 380 the emperor Theodosius took matters a step further by mandating the practice of Christianity throughout the empire. The clergy, who had once been reviled and persecuted, were now respected and even exalted. This newfound respect was welcome, of course, and it was the clergy's due as priests of Jesus Christ.

But clerical exaltation had a downside too. In fact, the empire so revered the clergy that the lay state began to seem insignificant by contrast. Historians speak of a widening gulf, at the end of the fourth century, between an elite celibate corps (of clergy and monks) and their passive congregations of married laity. As great a churchman as St. Jerome once quipped that he approved of marriage, but mostly because it was the breeding ground for future celibates. So it's little wonder that ordinary Christians began to lose sight of the sacramentality of marriage and their sacred vocation to family life and ordinary labor. The two-tiered spirituality created an artificial separation between the clergy and the laity—and thus between the

Church and the world. The distance between the two would only widen as the centuries wore on.

Indeed, at the time of Opus Dei's founding, the Church's canon law allowed for no institutional form that could accommodate close collaboration between clergy and laity. Organizations for priests were intended for priests, lay movements were intended for laity, and prior to the Second Vatican Council never the twain could meet in any integral, canonical sense.

So St. Josemaría accepted a number of temporary forms, confident that God would one day open a way for Opus Dei in the Church, a way that would be true to its foundational gifts (or "charisms"). He often said he was "giving in, but not giving up." As late as 1944 he wrote: "It is clear that, through our vocation, by our specific way of sanctifying ourselves and of working apostolically, we are a new pastoral phenomenon in the Church's life, although we are still as old as the Gospel."

Like the poet Robert Frost, Opus Dei had found "an old-fashioned way to be new." It took the Second Vatican Council, however, to find a newfangled way to recover the early-Christian vision promoted by St. Josemaría. In 1965, in the Council's "Decree on the Ministry and Life of Priests" *(Presbyterorum ordinis,* 10), the Church proposed a new institutional form, called the "personal prelature." Such an institution could accommodate both clergy and lay members cooperating to accomplish specific pastoral tasks. The word "personal" is what sets such an institution apart from particular churches. A personal prelature holds jurisdiction not over a geographic territory but over certain persons, wherever they may be.

In 1982 Pope John Paul II established Opus Dei as the Church's first personal prelature. (As I go to press, it is still the only one.) In the apostolic constitution *Ut sit,* Pope John Paul described the Work as "an apostolic organism made up of priests and lay people, both men and women, that is at the same time organic and undivided, that is to say, as an institution endowed with a unity of spirit, of aims, of government and of formation."

The theologian Rodríguez wrote: "The Church's richness . . . knows many forms of gathering and community, diverse ways for Christians to relate to one another." And that is certainly true. A personal prelature is something quite different from a religious order, or a particular church, or a lay movement. Yet all these forms receive their dignity from God and retain their special place in His Church.

Family Matters

I am a theologian, and so I have a certain academic interest in these questions of institutional form and foundational charism. I have to admit, though, that I have met few members of Opus Dei who share this peculiar interest. For most members, life in Opus Dei is life in a family. And just as you don't need a degree in family law to keep a happy home, you don't need to be fluent in canon law to live your vocation in the Church.

Rodríguez describes Opus Dei as "a family within the great *familia Dei* of the Church." That is, in fact, how I experienced Opus Dei from my first encounter. It struck me, for example, that some celibate members—called "numeraries"—lived together in centers that were run like family homes. They addressed their prelate not as "Bishop" but as "Father," because that was his place in the great household. St. Josemaría often referred to Opus Dei as both "a family and an army," and that always reminded me of the Old Testament, where God's family, the people of Israel, functioned as both a national family and a military force. What united them as both was *the covenant,* the divine decree that established the Israelites' kinship with each other and with God.

As I grew in my Christian faith, I grew also in my sense that I belonged to the *am 'Yahweh,* the Family of God. Yet within the national family of ancient Israel there were many tribes, and there are still many "tribes" in the Church today—a rich diversity of forms of Christian life. In ancient Israel, each tribe had a different role to play within the nation and the kingdom. Church life today is little different. In my early days as a Catholic, I would often ask the Lord: *Which tribe is mine?* And surely in answer to my prayer He led me not only to the Catholic Church but to Opus Dei. He leads others to other families within the family, other tribes in the nation, to the places where He wills.

Rome Sweet Home

When we strive to live faithfully, when we strive to make our work holy, then wherever we go, God goes with us. He is with us always, unto the close of the age, and to the ends of the earth. We serve the Church best by working with human perfection and offering that work as a holy sacrifice to God. Keep this in mind whenever you see photographs of the graves of the earliest Christians. They are decorated not with the cross but with a plow, a vineyard, an ax, a boat, a meal upon a table—the things of ordinary life. They were signs not of secularism but of secularity. Those symbols proclaimed to all the world that the kingdom had come, that the tools of every trade were accomplishing the work of God, and so also the work of the Church.

St. Josemaría lived to serve the Church. When he moved to Rome in 1946, he spent the entire night in prayer, gazing at the papal apartment in the distance. He could not bear the thought of acting contrary to the mission of the Church. "The only ambition, the only desire of Opus Dei and of each of its daughters and sons," he said many times, "is to serve the Church as she wants to be served, within our specific divine vocation." He even went so far as to beg of God: "Lord, if Opus Dei is not here to serve the Church, destroy it!"

All the popes since Pius XII have recognized Opus Dei for its spirit of fidelity and service to the Church. Pope John XXIII and Pope Paul VI entrusted important apostolic tasks to St. Josemaría and the faithful of Opus Dei. Pope John Paul I, just before his election to the papacy, wrote a warm, affectionate tribute to the founder of the Work—an essay that grasped his place in history perhaps better than anything written before. Pope John Paul II established Opus Dei as the Church's first personal prelature. And Pope Benedict XVI, very early in his pontificate, added a statue of St. Josemaría to the company of great saints on the walls of St. Peter's Basilica.

St. Josemaría loved and served the Church, and the Church returned his love abundantly. When the founder died in 1975, more than one-third of the world's bishops petitioned the Vatican to begin the process for canonizing him a saint.

Members of the Work strive to imitate St. Josemaría as good children of Mother Church. And Opus Dei best serves the Church by faithfully fulfilling its foundational charism—by

pursuing and promoting holiness in the most ordinary circumstances of everyday life, lighting up the pathways of the earth
with faith and love.

It's a specific vocation in the Church, but in the wake of
Vatican II, it is "on message" and "on mission" for all the lay
members of Christ's faithful people. To serve the Church and
to serve the world are hardly contradictory or even separate
aims. The first prelate of Opus Dei, Bishop Alvaro del Portillo,
once wrote: "Love for the world and for the Church did not
constitute two separate things in the mind and heart of the
founder of Opus Dei."

Nor should they pose any contradiction to the minds and
hearts of Catholics today.

Chapter 5

Work and Worship:
The Plan of Life

When you bring order into your life your time
will multiply, and then you will be able to give
God more glory, by working more in His service.

—THE WAY, NO. 80

Some years ago, as researchers labored fever-
ishly to map the human genome, one of the
leaders of the project permitted himself a brief
break to be interviewed by a reporter. Since he
was already a Nobel Prize winner—having
achieved that milestone in his youth—his time
was extremely valuable, not only to his colleagues but also to his country. Ever since the
discovery of mankind's basic genetic material,
all the developed nations of the world were in
competition, rushing to be the first to crack
the code. The media hyped a range of possible
outcomes: the eradication of many killer dis-
eases, the cloning of mice and men, the creation of new breeds of crops and livestock, the
manufacture of replacement limbs and organs,
and the greatest but most elusive promise of

all those long hours in the laboratory—bodily immortality. It's difficult to imagine more exalted material goals than these, measured against any purely earthly standard.

The Nobel Prize winner was, understandably, breathless as he spoke with the reporter about the work of his team of researchers. "So much is happening so fast," he said, "that we are in a constant state of excitement and hardly have time to think."

To careful readers, that line was chilling. Here was a team of brilliant men applying the whole of their lives to a work fraught with consequences and tangled in ambiguities—and they had no time to ponder those consequences or sort out the ambiguities.

No matter what work we do, our actions have consequences, and the world turns on those consequences. In my high school physics class, I learned Newton's third law: that every action has an equal and opposite reaction. That by itself would be a sobering thought. Now, moreover, physicists tell us that a change in a butterfly's flight pattern in Honduras can affect the weather in New York City. Our actions, then, even in the natural order, can produce outsized reactions. Even though you and I might be working at tasks more humble than the Human Genome Project, we should be deliberate about our work. We should work with recollection. We should make the time to stop and think. We should make the effort to be contemplative.

Resisting a Rest

Any discussion of a "work ethic" in our day and age must confront the problem of workaholism. And God knows it's a problem. From the beginning of creation, He built safeguards against this human tendency to overwork. He Himself rested on the seventh day. In the Decalogue, He commanded: "Six days shall work be done, but the seventh day is a Sabbath of solemn rest, holy to the Lord" (Exodus 31:15). In hallowing the Sabbath, the seventh day, He ensured that work would be ordered to worship, and also that work would proceed from worship. Eternity became a fixed point of contemplation, against which humankind could measure its past labors and future plans. God ordained that we should always have time to stop and think.

We, however, have become stuck in creation's sixth day, unable to get perspective on life, unable to get a decent rest. We have succumbed to the materialism of Revelation's beast, marked repeatedly by the sixth day—666—perpetually returning to the world of the workweek, like Bill Murray's character in the movie *Groundhog Day*.

Each year we welcome the invention of dozens of new labor-saving devices. Yet these devices—the cell phone, the teleconference, the PDA—can have the effect of extending the workday well into our time in the car and our precious hours at home, distracting us from the family, the scenery, and the road ahead of us.

If we do not obey the command to keep holy the Lord's day—if we do not make time to stop and think—we lose our ability to sense God's being and His presence, and we are left unable to worship Him. Still, we are wired for worship, and we must worship something. So we worship our work, and we consider worship to be the worst sort of work: pure drudgery.

My European friends are sometimes eager to point out the barbarity of American society, with its severely limited number of holidays. But Europeans are hardly better off: though they dutifully skip out of work on the great feast days, they are hardly filling their churches. They have come to worship leisure as much as Americans worship work. This is kind of like loving one's wedding day mostly because of the nice weather and the good food.

Again, if we fail to follow the rhythm God built into creation—the cosmic order of work and worship—we end up with a life disfigured and short on actual living. The "working for the weekend" attitude I mentioned earlier has now extended itself to the course of a lifetime. Investment advisers I know tell me of a common phenomenon they encounter: men who work maniacally to save for a lavish retirement, and then drop dead as soon as they stop working. On a long Sabbath afternoon, they are as lost and helpless as fish suddenly washed ashore.

Work must have a righteous end. By "end" I mean not just a point of stopping, though that is a necessary component. I mean especially a righteous reason, an end that's worth our heroic means.

For this, only God will do. As certainly as we were created for work, we were ultimately created for worship. Those are the bookends of human creation in the Book of Genesis. Work must lead to worship. Work must flow from worship. And work must be permeated by worship.

Professionalitis

St. Josemaría diagnosed this tendency to overwork as a sickness of the spirit. That was before the word "workaholism" was coined. St. Josemaría called the condition "professionalitis"—

suggesting a corruption of something good. As *appendicitis* is a rotting infection of the appendix, so *professionalitis* is the degradation of true professionalism. He counseled people to "put your professional interests in their place: they are only means to an end; they can never be regarded—in any way—as if they were the basic thing. These attacks of professionalitis are an obstacle to your union with God!"

Without worship, work becomes disordered. Worship, like work, is a basic human need. Both must be cultivated in proper proportion.

The danger, of course, is in overcompensation. In resting from hard work, workaholics often want to do nothing. But leisure—lived in the spirit of prayer and contemplation—is *most certainly not* doing nothing. It's an activity. It's a pursuit. It's doing *something*.

St. Josemaría wrote: "I have always seen rest as time set aside from daily tasks, never as days of idleness. Rest means re-cuperation: to gain strength, form ideals and make plans. In other words it means a change of occupation, so that you can come back later with a new impetus to your daily job."

The active celebration of the Day of the Lord is what makes our everyday work worthwhile. The Lord's Day moves professional fulfillment into the realm of possibility.

A Little Sunday in Every Day

Members of Opus Dei follow that rhythm in their week, but they also build it into their everyday lives. St. Josemaría advised Christians to build a Sabbath sense into every day of the week. He often said that he wanted laypeople to become "contemplatives in the middle of the world." To achieve this, he capitalized on one of the traditional frameworks of Catholic spirituality: the "plan of life."

The spirit of Opus Dei finds its strength in a program of standard prayers tailored to the unique circumstances of each individual. Every day an ordinary layperson can observe fixed times given to prayer of different varieties—silent conversation with God (mental prayer); the Mass (liturgical prayer); and the Morning Offering, Rosary, Angelus, and other recited (vocal) prayers. For members of Opus Dei—both married and celibate—these are "the norms," because they mark the milestones of a *normal* day. The basic plan, established by St. Josemaría, has undergone only small adjustments through the decades.

Morning Offering
Mental Prayer
Mass
Angelus
Rosary
Reading of the Gospel and some spiritual book
Some small act of penance
A short visit to the tabernacle
Preces (the daily prayers of Opus Dei)
Examination of conscience
Three Hail Marys at bedtime
The Sign of the Cross with holy water

There are a few other norms that are weekly, monthly, or annual—for example, weekly confession, a monthly day of recollection, and a yearly retreat.

When I first became a Catholic, I was unaccustomed to formal prayer. As an evangelical, I felt more at ease with spontaneous prayer, whether silent or vocalized. So I made an easy transition to the Catholic practice of mental prayer. The other forms, though, seemed daunting. And when I first saw a typical schedule of norms for an Opus Dei member, I thought I could never add so many new "tasks" to my day.

I had, however, a wise spiritual director and confessor, a priest who eased me into these practices one at a time. As I grew accustomed to the *Preces,* for example, it hardly seemed a "task." It was more like eating or reading—activities I've never had to struggle to perform! I found too that when I was faithful to my program, God "multiplied my time" (to steal another phrase from St. Josemaría): I managed to outperform my expectations, or sometimes I got an unexpected reprieve.

As I developed a plan of life, I began to experience greater peace in my days. At first, it was noticeable especially during my times of prayer, but gradually it seeped out to cover my work time as well, and then my conversations with my wife and children. I was more aware of God's company at all times, and I could rest in His presence. St. Augustine once defined peace as "tranquility in order." The plan of life is what finally imposed a spiritual order on my ordinary days. And that order was the necessary precondition of peace. My work at last was ordered to worship—and not only in my fondest intentions but, fairly often, in my conscious thought as well.

That was almost two decades ago. Sometimes, even after all these years, it is a struggle for me to fit everything into a busy day. But through the years I've noticed a pattern. I've noticed that when I'm faithful to my commitment to prayer, I'm at peace. When I let my norms go slack, I get anxious, uncertain, and scatterbrained. I depend on myself overly much, and I forget that God is my strength.

A plan is something that requires effort at the start but makes the rest of life less arduous. Now I find it hard to imagine living my busy life—as a husband, a dad, and a teacher—without the clear daily markers in my plan of life. I compare it to tennis. It's possible to play something *like* tennis on any smooth, hard surface. But the game is more true, more fun, and more satisfying on a court with clearly marked lines and a net.

Fidelity to the clear daily markers is key. St. Josemaría said: "You must above all stick to your daily periods of prayer, which should be fervent, generous and not cut short. And you must make sure that those minutes of prayer are not done only when you feel the need, but at fixed times, whenever it is possible. Don't neglect these details. If you subject yourself to this daily worship of God, I can assure you that you will be always happy."

I have friends who object to this approach. They believe that prayer, like love, should be spontaneous. They dismiss a plan of life as "checklist spirituality." I agree that spontaneous prayer is a wonderful thing, but lifelong love depends on certain rituals as well. My wife Kimberly never tires of hearing me say, "I love you" and "You're beautiful," no matter how often I repeat those phrases in a given week. She doesn't fault me for celebrating our marriage rather precisely on our anniversary. Nor did she complain at all, several years ago, when I suggested we start going out on a date together on a certain night every week. In love as in poetry, a certain fixed form makes spontaneity all the more possible and all the more poignant.

In less exalted matters too we follow a plan—and our lives would be unlivable without one. Every morning I follow pretty much the same schedule of basic hygiene, and I haven't considered it a burden since I was around ten years old. (Back then, like most little boys, I thought hygiene should be less rigid and more spontaneous.) My hygienic program, which I no longer notice, keeps me in relatively good health, and it makes my presence more bearable for my coworkers and family.

Rite at the Root

The most important element in Opus Dei's plan of life is the Holy Mass. For St. Josemaría, it was never just "the Mass," but always "the Holy Mass." And it's easy to see why. He described the eucharistic liturgy as "the most sacred and transcendent act which we, men and women, with God's grace can carry out in this life." He experienced the Mass as heaven on earth: "Receiving the Body and Blood of Our Lord is, in a certain sense, like loosening our ties with earth and time, so as to be already with God in heaven."

Members of Opus Dei strive to get to Mass every day. The Mass is like the sun around which the rest of the day revolves. St. Josemaría did not believe that the rest of the day is unimportant, but rather that everything else in life should derive its importance from the Mass.

Opus Dei's second prelate, Bishop Javier Echevarría, put it this way: "The presence of the Eucharist in a Christian's life is not limited to the sublime moment of the Mass. We can bring to the altar our daily actions, our ordinary tasks, as we strive throughout the day to refer them to God in the Eucharist. Any honorable work can be a means to unite ourselves spiritually to Christ's sacrifice in the Holy Mass."

That's what it's all about: our work ordered to our worship, our work raised up as sacrificial worship, our worship giving new life to our work. St. Josemaría put it well: "Keep struggling, so that the Holy Sacrifice of the Altar really becomes the center and the root of your interior life, and so your whole day will turn into an act of worship—an extension of the Mass you have attended and a preparation for the next. Your whole day will then be an act of worship."

This is how ordinary laypeople participate in the priesthood of Jesus Christ. Jesus presides over the great cosmic liturgy, and we are His concelebrants. He looks at the world the way He looks at the host when the priest pronounces the words: "This is My body." We offer the world to the Father with Christ the High Priest, and the world is transformed. This is the answer to our constant prayer: "Thy kingdom come." And the kingdom arrives as the work of our hands.

The Mass gives profound meaning to all our work when we place our work (by an interior act of prayer) on the altar of sacrifice. This was the heart and soul of the vision St. Josemaría had in 1928. In 1964 the Second Vatican Council made it a hallmark of the Church's teaching on the common priesthood of the laity. Speaking of ordinary Christians, the Council Fathers said:

> For their work, prayers and apostolic endeavors, their
> ordinary married and family life, their daily labor,
> their mental and physical relaxation, if carried out in
> the Spirit, and even the hardships of life if patiently

borne—all of these become spiritual sacrifices acceptable to God through Jesus Christ (cf. 1 Peter 2:5). During the celebration of the Eucharist these sacrifices are most lovingly offered to the Father along with the Lord's body. Thus as worshipers whose every deed is holy, the lay faithful consecrate the world itself to God.

Thus, our "Mass" is not ended when the priest says, "The Mass is ended." We live the transformation, the miracle, the communion, in every action of our day.

The great Rabbi Abraham Joshua Heschel said that the Sabbath is in time what the temple is in space. The plan of life inserts the spirit of the Lord's Day into every day of the week. It is a spirit of contemplation, making us "contemplatives in the middle of the world." As our Sabbath is always, so our temple is everywhere—because it is in heaven, and because our hearts are already in heaven.

This is precisely why we are *contemplatives*. A contemplative is, etymologically, a person who is busy about the activities associated *with the temple* ("con-temple-ative"). And what activities take place in the temple? Prayer and sacrifice. In the ancient world, shrines were for mere devotions, and temples were for sacrifice.

Today that's what all our lives are for—prayer and sacrifice. It sounds like a plan.

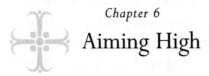

Chapter 6

Aiming High

Ambition: to be good myself, and to see everyone
else better than I.

—THE WAY, NO. 2

We should stand in awe of the dignity God has
given to our everyday loves and labors. He has
empowered us to offer them as holy sacrifices.
He has ordained us as priests to officiate at the
daily sacrifice—whether we are sitting at a
desk, standing at an assembly line, or leaning
over a diaper-changing table. We are a nation
of priests who "dwell in the house of the Lord,"
the holy temple, "all the days" of our lives (see
Psalm 27:4).

Thus, all the Bible's instructions, laws, and
meditations about sacrifice should take on a
new and profound meaning for us. For God received the fruits of human labor as sacrifice
since the earliest pages of Genesis, and he
showed great concern with the way his priests
made their offering. Think, for example, of the
story of Cain and Abel. Why did Abel's sacrifice please God while Cain's did not? Think too

of the laws of Exodus, Leviticus, and Deuteronomy. We tend to identify "the Law" of ancient Israel with the Ten Commandments, but the Decalogue takes up less than a chapter, while the prescriptions for sacrifice make up the bulk of the Bible's legislation.

It is fair for us to ask: why did God care so much about the quality of Israel's offerings? After all, He Himself pointed out that He did not need them as food.

Love and Sacrifice

God instituted sacrifice not for His own sake but for our sake. The sacrificial law is a means to God's glorious end: it disciplines His people, focusing their attention on worship, gratitude, sorrow for sin, the need for purity, and the necessity of renouncing everything in order to cling to God. Sacrifice is an expression of love, and it is a precondition of love. This is true of human love as well: even today, when a man and woman marry, they promise exclusive love, and they renounce the possibility of amorous encounters with all other men and women. They exchange rings made of precious metal and sometimes jewels as well. They make an offering of all that they have, all that they are, symbolized by the most valuable minerals the earth can produce.

God's law enabled His people to establish and maintain a loving relationship with their creator and redeemer. The ritual law required that the people bring forth for sacrifice the first fruits of their fields and orchards, the firstborn of their flocks and herds, and the best wine pressed from their vineyards. They were forbidden to choose less valuable items—sheep, goats, or bulls, for example, that were blemished or lame (see, for example, Leviticus 22:20–24).

Again, we have to remind ourselves that God made these laws for our sake, not for His. If He demanded the most valuable livestock, it was for Israel's sake, not for God's. It was because humanity, and every human family and every human being, needed then and needs now to give their best to God. He does not settle for second-best—and again, it is not because He needs our gifts or enjoys seeing His children deprived of good things. It is because He desires our love, given freely but completely.

We learn this lesson not only from the Law but from the prophets as well. The prophet Malachi rails against the priests of his time, who were offering God the dregs of the bustling economy and keeping the best for themselves. Through Malachi, God chastises them for "thinking that the Lord's table may be despised" (Malachi 1:7). That's strong language, but it rings true. A man who insists that he loves his wife while he lavishes the finest gifts upon his mistress does not truly love his wife.

Through Malachi, God asks the priests of the Jerusalem Temple: "When you offer blind animals in sacrifice, is that no evil? And when you offer those that are lame or sick, is that no evil? Present that to your governor; will he be pleased with you or show you favor?" (Malachi 1:8–9).

He points out that they give to God such shoddy service as they would never dare to give to the Persian governor. Yet God is all-seeing, all-knowing, and all-powerful; unlike the Persian governor, He cannot be fooled. What does that say about the faith of Israel's priests? About their reverence? About their awe in the presence of the Lord?

What human beings offer to God is symbolic, but it is not merely a token. It matters what symbols we choose; it matters what gifts we offer. Yes, it's the thought that counts, but the gift should be an expression of the thought that is as clear and as pure as possible. If a priest offered to God a victim that was less than the best, he deserved all the invective that Malachi could muster (with divine inspiration).

The implications for us should be self-evident. We daily stand as priests who offer our work to God. We should offer Him only the best we have. We should always wish to offer Him something greater, purer, and more perfect. In all our labors, we should strive toward this end.

Saintly Striving

This is the engine behind what St. Josemaría called "holy ambition." And it is easy to distinguish this sort of ambition from the less noble varieties. Driven by holy ambition, we serve God and others. Driven by petty ambition, we serve only ourselves. St. Josemaría put it well: "Those who are 'ambitious,' with small, personal, miserable ambitions, cannot understand that the friends of God should seek to achieve something through a spirit of service and without such 'ambition.' "

We should never confuse Christian humility and modesty with a will to underachieve. Jesus commanded us not to hide our lights under a bushel. He told us we are a city set on a hill. Well, first we have to take the hill, through our efforts at honest work, aided by God's grace.

The Church echoes the Master in these matters. The Second Vatican Council urged Catholics to "better themselves through human labors." For if we improve our own lot, we will be able to help more and more of our fellow citizens. The laity "should raise all of society, and even creation itself, to a better mode of existence. Indeed, they should imitate by their lively charity, in their joyous hope and by their voluntary sharing of each others' burdens, the very Christ who plied His hands with carpenter's tools and who in union with His Father, is continually working for the salvation of all men. In this, then, their daily work they should climb to the heights of holiness and apostolic activity." That's a summons for Catholics to reach high in their professional work. And it's a clear indication that the drive to succeed professionally and the Christian vocation to holiness are complementary motives—or at least they can be.

In another document, the Second Vatican Council made the connection stronger still. It deserves to be quoted at length:

> Throughout the course of the centuries, men have labored to better the circumstances of their lives through a monumental amount of individual and collective effort. To believers, this point is settled: considered in itself, this human activity accords with God's will. For man, created to God's image, received a mandate to subject to himself the earth and all it contains, and to govern the world with justice and holiness; a mandate to relate himself and the totality of things to Him Who was to be acknowledged as the Lord and Creator of all. Thus, by the subjection of all things to man, the name of God would be wonderful in all the earth.
>
> This mandate concerns the whole of everyday activity as well. For while providing the substance of life for themselves and their families, men and

women are performing their activities in a way which appropriately benefits society. They can justly consider that by their labor they are unfolding the Creator's work, consulting the advantages of their brother men, and are contributing by their personal industry to the realization in history of the divine plan.

Thus, far from thinking that works produced by man's own talent and energy are in opposition to God's power, and that the rational creature exists as a kind of rival to the Creator, Christians are convinced that the triumphs of the human race are a sign of God's grace and the flowering of His own mysterious design. For the greater man's power becomes, the farther his individual and community responsibility extends. Hence it is clear that men are not deterred by the Christian message from building up the world, or impelled to neglect the welfare of their fellows, but that they are rather more stringently bound to do these very things.

Industry, talent, energy, responsibility, triumph—that is the language of ambition and achievement. It is a language that the children of God should speak fluently, and their talk should reflect their daily walk.

For God's Eyes Only

Surprisingly, St. Josemaría talks about this ambition in terms not so much of grand schemes as of "little things." He wrote:

"Reject any ambition for honors. Think instead about your duties, how to do them well and the instruments you need to accomplish them. In this way, you will not hanker for position, and if one comes you will see it just as it is: a burden to bear in the service of souls."

We should not, then, be so distracted by our long-term goals that we neglect the seemingly routine and insignificant tasks that require our attention today. We find God's will in the small tasks that others are depending on us to complete. We find God's will even—and perhaps especially—in the little things we do that no one ever notices. Since these are "for God's eyes only," they can rise as a pure sacrifice—when they're done well, done on time, and offered to God.

There are benefits too in the natural order. For if we do these little things promptly and carefully, without procrastinating and with our full attention, we'll find that we're moving further toward our professional goals, even as we're fulfilling the obligations of charity and justice. Indeed, it is ludicrous for us to think we can accomplish great things if we're not keeping up with the minutiae. St. Josemaría wrote to one correspondent: "You tell me: when the chance comes to do something big, then! . . . Then? Are you seriously trying to convince me—and to convince yourself—that you will be able to win in the supernatural Olympics without daily preparation, without training?"

Careful attention to little things is a human virtue so basic that it seems hardly worth uttering. Can anyone in the modern age really improve on Benjamin Franklin's cautionary tale? "For want of a nail the shoe was lost; for want of a shoe the horse was lost; and for want of a horse the rider was lost; being overtaken and slain by the enemy, all for want of care about a horse-shoe nail." We all know that failure of duty in small matters can have unintended and disastrous consequences.

The Catholic approach, however, offers something more. Indeed, it spells the difference between doing human work and doing God's work. This does not supersede Ben Franklin's purely natural considerations, but raises them to a supernatural perfection. It is a commonplace of Catholic theology that God's grace does not destroy what He created in nature, but builds upon it, completes it, and elevates it. So the ordinary believer should take the most ordinary events—passing a car on the highway, shucking corn, responding to e-mail—and, doing them well by human standards, raise them up to the divine standard by offering them to God, who will bring them to completion according to His holy will. "You have the power to transform everything human into something divine," said St. Josemaría, "just as King Midas turned everything he touched into gold!"

Get to Work

The little things we do are the building blocks of the big things God has planned, in our lives, in history, and in the spinning out of the cosmos.

Indeed, little things matter so much to us because they matter so much to God. That is the plain meaning of Jesus's parable of the talents (Matthew 25:14–31)—a parable of ambition. Twice in that parable Jesus portrays the master (representing God) as saying, "Well done, good and faithful servant; you have been faithful over a little, I will set you over much; enter into the joy of your master."

It's the little things that count, even for God. For in our attention to little things, we imitate Him most perfectly. Our God is the master of the universe, whose mind and power are evident in the formation of the Himalayas, but also in the movement of subatomic particles. And He doesn't move mountains without moving a whole lot of electrons in the process!

Thus, there is a hidden grandeur in the most ordinary things. St. Josemaría saw this, and he had little patience for those would-be saints with romantic inclinations who saw ordinary life as merely an obstacle to true greatness. He called this attitude "mystical wishful thinking." We should not sit around whining: "If only I hadn't married; if only I had a different job or qualification; if only I were in better health; if only I were younger; if only I were older." Instead, St. Josemaría said, we should "turn to the most material and immediate reality"— and get to work.

The smallest tasks can take on *infinite* value when we offer them to God, when we carry them out as works of God. Holy ambition strives for greatness even in little things, but it is content with the earthly results that God wills or permits.

Thus, we can live with holy ambition even if our professional prospects are few. In holy ambition, there is none of the anxiety, disappointment, and dissatisfaction that cling to men and women as they strive to climb the corporate or social ladder. Holy ambition hopes for great things, but contents itself with whatever God wills. St. Josemaría urged Christians: "Do not lose that holy ambition of yours to lead the whole world to God, but . . . remember that you too have to be obedient and work away at that obscure job, which does not seem at all brilliant, for as long as God asks nothing else of you. He has His own times and paths."

An Elite Corps of Everybody

Holy ambition is something we can practice no matter where we are or what we do. It is an idea that I found enormously attractive when I first discovered Opus Dei. At the time, some critics were accusing Opus Dei of elitism and exclusivity. I found the whole thing rather amusing because my friends in Opus Dei always had time for me—and I was a tenuously employed ex-Protestant minister with no clear direction in his career. I was hardly the kind of person who could be counted among "the elite." One day I distracted myself by making a list of my long-term goals. Chief among them was my fond wish to teach a parish adult education class someday. This isn't what most cultural elites would call a hyperactive ambition. The charge of exclusivism was even funnier: I wasn't even Catholic.

Around the same time, my good friend John Haas was an ex-Protestant minister working in a more elite field, international banking, and he traveled halfway around the world to discover Opus Dei's holy ambition at work. But he found it in a surprising place. John fondly recalls his encounter with a Guatemalan cab driver named Gustavo, who drove his jalopy swiftly but safely, negotiating curves and corners with utmost precision, consistently delivering his passenger on time to every destination, no matter how remote. John marveled at the poor man's skill and conscientiousness. He was equally impressed with the man's obvious love for his wife and children, who regularly emerged as pleasant subjects in his conversation. At some point, John asked him about the spiritual sources of that love. Gustavo "pulled down the visor of his beat-up, dusty old car and pulled out a prayer card to Josemaría Escrivá."

That's hardworking ambition, but it's also holy ambition that leaves the results to God. "Have you seen how that imposing building was built? One brick upon another. Thousands. But one by one. And bags of cement, one by one. And blocks of stone, each of them insignificant compared with the massive whole. And beams of steel. And men working, the same hours, day after day. . . . Have you seen how that imposing building was built? . . . By dint of little things!"

This is not elitism—though I'm quite sure that many, many people who look at life this way manage to go very far in their professional life. People who work for love are highly motivated workers. And when their ultimate motivation is love for God, their works can be so great as to shape the course of world events. The history textbooks bear ample witness to this. Moreover, a spirituality that takes human ambition into account will be extremely attractive to those Christians who are ambitious by nature. It makes divine sense of the drive they feel pressing them onward, and it helps them channel that drive in a healthy way.

Like most of what we find in the spirit of Opus Dei, this is mere Catholicism, though the emphasis is uniquely St. Josemaría's. The Vatican's *Compendium of the Social Doctrine of the Church* teaches that "everyone should make legitimate use of his talents to contribute to the abundance that will benefit all, and to harvest the just fruits of his labor." If we believe this to be true, then we won't hesitate to ask for a raise or a promotion when these are our due.

What's more, we must look upon our raises and promotions as not only our just deserts but *God's* just deserts. Ponder another passage from the Church's *Compendium:* "By means of work, man governs the world with God; together with God he is its lord and accomplishes good things for himself and for others." By "man" that passage means you and me—every Christian man, woman, and child. We govern "together with God" in the place where we find ourselves, and for God's sake and for the sake of His kingdom, we should always wish to better ourselves.

Sunrise, Sunset

In the spirit of Opus Dei, holy ambition is not self-aggrandizement, not a free pass for overachievers. It is an acknowledgment that we will be judged by how well we use the time and talent God has given us. It is an acknowledgment that our work, however small and humble, undergoes a transformation when we place it on the altar of God.

Our everyday work might seem like just one little thing after another, but so are the bread and wine that the priest consecrates at every Mass. It is the offering—in Greek, the *anaphora*—that makes them the Body, Blood, Soul, and Divinity of Jesus Christ. In a similar way, our works are transformed by our priestly offering, our "Midas touch," into something divine.

Think back to those words of the prophet Malachi when he exhorted Jerusalem's priests to purify their offerings. Today those words are addressed to us. God wants us to offer Him our best efforts at work. Why should we make an offering of work that is blemished or hobbled if God has given us gifts to do better?

Malachi's exhortation is just a prelude to the biblical

prophecy that the Fathers of the Church applied—more than any other prophecy—to the Holy Mass. "For from the rising of the sun to its setting My name is great among the nations, and in every place incense is offered to My name, and a pure offering; for My name is great among the nations, says the Lord of hosts" (Malachi 1:11). Today that prophecy echoes in the Third Eucharistic Prayer of the Latin rite: "so that from east to west a perfect offering may be made, to the glory of Your name."

That line on the map, from east to west, from sunrise to sunset, cuts right through our ordinary lives, wherever we may be. Wherever we may be, that's the place where we're called to make a pure offering, a perfect offering. For the sacrifice of our working life and our family life is one with the sacrifice of the Mass.

People said of Jesus, "He does all things well" (Mark 7:37). Here's my hope, my prayer, my holy ambition: may they be able to say the same thing about me someday, and about you, and about all of us who bear the name of God in baptism. May we glorify that name by our lives.

Chapter 7

Friendship and Confidence

Those well-timed words, whispered into the ear
of your wavering friend; the helpful conversation
that you managed to start at the right moment;
the ready professional advice that improves his
university work; the discreet indiscretion by
which you open up unexpected horizons for
his zeal. This all forms part of the "apostolate
of friendship."

—THE WAY, NO. 846

Spreading the love of Jesus Christ is a duty of
all Christians. We can't keep our faith unless
we give it away. We all share in the Church's
responsibility to evangelize. To use the technical terms of the teaching Church: there is
a universal call to the *apostolate*. So Jesus's
great commission to the Apostles applies to
each and all of us Christians: "Go therefore and
make disciples of all nations, baptizing them in
the name of the Father and of the Son and of
the Holy Spirit, teaching them to observe
all that I have commanded you" (Matthew
28:19–20).

The laity must bear much of the burden of Christ's command. For we are the Catholics whose work and migrations take us to all nations. Our special duty is the sanctification of the world, a duty that was taken up joyfully and executed rather successfully by the first generations of Christians. It was to these "early Christians" that St. Josemaría always looked for inspiration and instruction. For they lived in a hostile and perverse culture during a time of intense persecution of Christians. The Church owned no buildings and conducted no public events. And still Christians managed to convert the Roman empire. Throughout almost three centuries of persecution, the Church grew at a steady rate of 40 percent per decade!

The Catholic Church had many holy and heroic popes during those years. Many of them died as martyrs, and most have been canonized as saints. We must not underestimate the value of their witness and the graces they won by the blood they shed. But we must also realize that, given the primitive state of communications in the ancient world, many Christians might not have even known the name of the current pope at a given moment, and it might have taken months for the news of a papal death or succession to reach the rural backwaters in the provinces. In the meantime, ordinary Christians went on living their lives, working their land, trading their wares, and raising their families. Through all of this activity, they witnessed to their Catholic faith, and they won over their neighbors.

They evangelized. Yet they did it in a way far different from our modern stereotypes of Christian behavior. They were not "Bible-thumpers," though they loved the Word of God. They didn't drag along reluctant friends every time they went to church services; the Mass, in those days, was a closed affair, conducted in private homes, and open to members only.

Soul of the World

The early Christians succeeded in a quiet way, sanctifying the world from within, like yeast in the dough. The second-century *Letter to Diognetus* put it beautifully: "As the soul is in the body, so Christians are in the world. The soul is dispersed through all the members of the body, and Christians are scattered through all the cities of the world. . . . The invisible soul is guarded by the visible body, and Christians are known indeed to be in the world, but their godliness remains invisible."

It was a seemingly invisible work of the Church. For Christians were not doing anything out of the ordinary. They weren't wearing a distinctive uniform or behaving oddly in public places. The *Letter to Diognetus* explained: "Christians are distinguished from others neither by country, nor language, nor the customs they observe. For they neither inhabit cities of their own, nor use a peculiar form of speech, nor lead a life which is marked out by anything unusual. . . . But, inhabiting Greek as well as barbarian cities . . . and following the customs of the natives in respect to clothing, food, and the rest of their ordinary conduct, they display to us their wonderful and striking way of life."

So successful were our Christian ancestors that the pagan authorities often accused them of relying on magic, secrecy, and a vast web of conspirators to accomplish their ends. Their success seemed too great to be chalked up to ordinary human means. The African Christian Tertullian noted: "We began just yesterday, and already we fill the world and all your places: the cities, the islands, the towns, the municipalities, the councils, even the army camps, the tribunals, the assemblies, the palace, the senate, and the forum. We have left you only your temples!"

Yet so it was: they converted the world by doing their work—and by doing God's work, which came down to the same thing. They conquered not by military means, or by covert means, and certainly not by preaching. Instead, in the words of the Second Vatican Council, ordinary lay Christians made "Christ known to others, especially by the testimony of a life resplendent in faith, hope, and charity."

St. Josemaría exhorted ordinary Christians to carry out the same kind of quiet but effective evangelization today. He called it the "apostolate of friendship and confidence."

Friendship is, after all, the ordinary social bond between people. Confidence and trust are the cement in everyday professional relationships. Only on the basis of friendship and confidence can ordinary Christians give a credible, full-time witness to the claims of Christianity.

For our ordinary apostolate must be personal. It must be individual, person to person. This is the only way we can realistically fulfill the Church's universal call to the apostolate. The alternative is to hanker forever after doing mass-market evangelism, for which we might never have time. One corporate executive faced this spiritual crisis and went on a pilgrimage to Calcutta, India, to seek the advice of Mother Teresa. She spoke sharply with him. She told him to go back home to Wisconsin and be a good CEO so that his company might prosper and keep many people gainfully employed. "Bloom where you're planted," she told him, so that in Milwaukee the Missionaries of Charity would never find "the poorest of the poor."

Friendship and confidence: this is the way the early Christians carried out their apostolate, and it worked so well that they were accused of all manner of secret powers and vast conspiracies.

Friendship and confidence are the distinguishing marks of Opus Dei's apostolate today—not institutional programs or public demonstrations, though these things do have their place. Opus Dei does sponsor regular events such as retreats, evenings of recollection, study circles, and doctrine classes, but even these are not usually advertised or publicized. The preferred method of "spreading the word" is by person-to-person contact: friendship.

It all comes down to handshakes and heart-to-hearts.

Mission: Impossible

There is, of course, not a lot of earthly glory or religious romance in this workaday apostolate. St. Josemaría acknowledged this: "I'll place a martyrdom within your reach: to be an apostle and not call yourself an apostle, to be a missionary— with a mission—and not call yourself a missionary, to be a man of God and to seem a man of the world: to pass unnoticed."

Our proverbial backyard, then, is our mission field. And God has sent us out to everyone we meet. "Out of a hundred souls," St. Josemaría said, "we are interested in a hundred." That means all the members of our family, all our coworkers, all our neighbors. Everyone on earth needs to draw closer to God, and that need will be with them as long as they're alive on this earth. God sends us into so many lives as His instrument, His voice, His shepherd's staff and crook. He sends us even to those Christians who are holier and more virtuous than we are. They too need to draw closer to Him as long as they're alive on earth. Our unworthiness doesn't matter. In fact, it's a given! We do not deserve to be called by God, and humanly speaking, we cannot possibly carry out the work He wants us to do. We must, however, come to realize that the apostolate is not *our* work, but *God's* work—quite literally, *Opus Dei*. And "nothing is impossible with God" (Luke 1:38). "I can do all things in Him who strengthens me" (Philippians 4:13).

Thus, our apostolate must always begin with prayer. We should look for opportunities to speak with our friends about Jesus Christ. But we should first take many opportunities to speak with Jesus Christ about our friends. We should ask Him to show us our friends' needs, so that we might lend a hand and serve their true and immediate needs. The stuff of our apostolate might be the well-timed gift of a prepared meal, the offer of babysitting, the ride across town. When we show kindness to our friends, we manifest the love of Christ, even if we don't reveal our deepest motives. We need not be like television shows that announce, "This kindness has been brought to you by the grace of Jesus Christ." Our friends will value our kindness in itself. As they get to know us better, they will discover the divine source of our kindnesses, and they may come to value that divine source even more than the sum of all our particular kindnesses.

The source must always be our deep encounter with Christ, and our identification with Him. We pray to Him, and we offer our life in atonement, as He did. This is, at least partly, what St. Josemaría meant when he spoke of "sanctifying others through work." We offer our work as a sacrifice, for the sake of others, and thus, in our daily struggles, we win graces for them in their struggles.

St. Josemaría sketched out a simple apostolic program: "First, prayer; then, atonement; in the third place, very much 'in the third place,' action." Most of our apostolate, then, will be invisible. Our friends might someday glimpse the tip of the iceberg—maybe. In heaven, however, they'll know our love in its very depths.

Apostolic Goals

What does this apostolate look like? For me, one of the most vivid images comes from the violent years just before the Spanish Civil War. As political power shifted first one way and then another, social relations broke down. Trust reached a low point; personal betrayals were routine events. Citizens across the political spectrum—from anarchists to monarchists—found themselves thrown together in the crowded jails. Often the cell blocks erupted in violence from the mutual hatred of the political opponents. Once, in 1932, St. Josemaría visited some young friends who were political prisoners. He listened as they vented their fury about having to spend their days in such close company with their enemies. His advice was clear: they should make friends out of their enemies. They listened to him and organized soccer teams—not republicans versus anarchists, but mixed squads, each of which included a range of political opinion. The idea worked. One of the anarchists observed that he had never played such a clean soccer game. Many of the players remained friends long after their jail terms came to an end, and some of the anarchists eventually returned to the practice of the Catholic faith.

St. Josemaría often spoke eloquently about the effects of this apostolic approach: "May you sow peace and joy on all sides. May you not say a disturbing word to anyone. May you know how to walk arm-in-arm with those who do not think as you do. May you never mistreat anyone. May you be brothers to all and sowers of peace and joy." Yet, as his successor Bishop Javier Echevarría noted, the founder "never failed to point out that this Christian coexistence does not mean yielding to error, to false doctrine."

In true friendship, we have the freedom to speak a word of correction or even reproof. In the wake of prayer, we have the ability to say it in a diplomatic way. Truth can move mountains without employing rhetorical explosives.

The apostolate of friendship and confidence worked for the early Church. What impressed the ancient Romans about Christianity was not so much its arguments, or its art, or its literature—but its love. "See how they love one another," the pagans marveled. Tertullian noted that the pure quality of Christian love stood out in the Roman world because the Romans experienced so little in the way of friendship and trust. Theirs was a promiscuously adulterous society, and both men and women dared not turn their back to their friends. But the Christians were different.

What worked for our Christian forebears will work for us

today. Apostolate must be made up of personal and disinterested love if it's ever to succeed. Friendship moves hearts more surely than the best sales techniques and evangelistic gimmicks that church committees can manufacture.

Of that I have personal experience—and in it great confidence.

Chapter 8

Secularity and Secularism

Be men and women of the world, but don't be
worldly men and women.

—THE WAY, NO. 939

An American comedian, some years back,
drew laughter from his late-night audiences by
imitating a televangelist. Whenever he used
the word *secular,* he would hiss it out as if it
were the byword of the demonic serpent in
the Garden of Eden. It rang true as satire. The
word *secular,* for some Christians, represents
the source and sum of evil in the world. *Secular* is, for these Christians, the very opposite of
sacred.

It's easy to see how such ideas arise. The
revolutionary movements of the eighteenth and
nineteenth centuries intentionally placed those
terms in opposition. Secular affairs were matters of the public interest. Religion, the realm
of the sacred, was a private affair of the individual conscience. In some places, this notion
manifested itself as a separation of church and
state. Other countries, however, went beyond

separation to suppression, declaring that since religion is a private matter, it should be restricted to the private sphere, never to influence public discussion or policy. This took various extreme forms. In Mexico, for example, priests were at first forbidden to wear clerical attire in public; later they were forbidden to exercise their priesthood at all. In France, more recently, a law forbade Muslim girls to wear head scarves in public schools. In my country, we have an extremely odd situation: cities are forbidden to display crèches in public spaces during the Christmas season, but artists receive government grants for works that deface religious icons.

It is a short step from separation to suppression, and it's that historically inevitable movement that puts the hiss in the comedian's pronunciation of *secular.*

When religion is sentenced to house arrest, then the "secular" has itself become a religion, rightly called "secularism."

Had We But World Enough and Time

But secularism forces a false dichotomy on societies and individuals. St. Josemaría put it well: "Religion cannot be separated from life, either in theory or in daily reality." In Christian thinking, *sacred* and *secular* denote two distinct but not separate orders. The word *secular* derives from the Latin *saecula;* meaning both "the world" and "the ages," it encompasses everything in the space-time continuum, everything in creation. Thus, traditional Latin blessings and prayers often end with the phrase "per omnia saecula saeculorum," meaning simultaneously "throughout the entire world" and "through all the ages of ages." An ordinary Christian blessing, then, consecrates the world and all that's in it. This is the extension in history of that most famous of Gospel passages: "God so loved the world. . . . For God sent the Son into the world, not to condemn the world, but that the world might be saved through him" (John 3:16–17).

The Church does not despise the secular. A Catholic layman should not despise the world. In fact, the life of the lay Catholic is God's answer to the traditional prayer of blessings on *"omnia saecula saeculorum."*

Here, however, we must make a distinction—between the lay vocation and the vocation to vowed-religious life. The religious vocation is by nature a call to separate oneself from the world. Religious priests, monks, sisters, and brothers follow a certain path to holiness that leads them away from worldly affairs. They renounce marriage, property, and freedom. They embrace, to some degree, an attitude that spiritual literature calls "contempt for the world" *(contemptus mundi)*. In the words of St. Clare of Assisi, they leave the things of time for the things of eternity. They set themselves apart, both for the sake of their own salvation and so that their prayers might sanctify the world. Monks and nuns practice a flight from the world, and they remedy the evils of the world from afar. Often, a religious order's dress code—its habit—further distinguishes its members from the ordinary run of humanity.

The lay Christian, on the other hand, is called to sanctify the world from within. The distinguishing mark of lay men and women is their "secular character," an orientation that is sometimes called "secularity." Lay Catholics need not leave the things of time in order to find the things of eternity. "Heaven and earth seem to merge on the horizon," St. Josemaría said. "But where they really meet is in your hearts, when you sanctify your everyday lives." The temporal order is God's domain, and so it is the domain of His children as well. The *Catechism* cites the Second Vatican Council in this regard: "By reason of their special vocation it belongs to the laity to seek the Kingdom of God by engaging in temporal affairs and directing them according to God's will." The *Code of Canon Law* lays it down that the laity's mission is "to permeate and perfect the temporal order of things with the spirit of the Gospel."

St. Josemaría drew the necessary contrasts between secular and religious spiritualities and emphasized that "secularity" is essential for Opus Dei priests as well, since they are "secular priests" and not members of a religious order. They do not take vows. "Nothing distinguishes my children from their fellow citizens. On the other hand, apart from the Faith they share, they have nothing in common with the members of religious congregations. I love the religious, and venerate and admire their apostolates, their cloister, their separation from the world, their *contemptus mundi,* which are other signs of holiness in the Church. But the Lord has not given me a religious vocation, and for me to desire it would be a disorder. No authority on earth can force me to be a religious, just as no authority can force me to marry. I am a secular priest: a priest of Jesus Christ who is passionately in love with the world."

A Way with the World

Secularism doesn't arise out of nowhere. It sometimes emerges as an overreaction to a real abuse of religious authority. The abuse might be official, as when a state or a political party claims that its approach is the only valid Catholic approach. Throughout history there have been disastrous examples of rulers who invoked approval from God or the Church when they lacked persuasive arguments, good reasons, or popular support. History also tells of some priests and hierarchs who used their pulpits or other symbols of their ecclesiastical authority to exert undue influence over business or political matters—matters that were actually morally neutral.

The name for this abuse is clericalism, and it seems inevitably to provoke a wave of anticlericalism. There are few human desires so ugly as the lust for power, and it is especially unbecoming in men who are ordained for service. The clergy holds a certain authority in matters of the Church's discipline. But exercising that authority is a delicate operation. Their office deserves respect, but clergy should expect deference only in matters where they have legitimate authority. Our clergy may tell us when we must go to Mass, or whom we may validly marry, but they shouldn't be dictating our choice of restaurants or political parties. (Their authority extends to party membership, however, when the parties themselves have become essentially immoral. At various times, Catholic bishops have legitimately forbidden membership in political associations affiliated with Nazism, communism, and freemasonry.)

Nor should laypeople act toward the hierarchy in an obsequious or overly deferential way. Corporate CEOs have no business running their companies' strategic plans past the local pastor. When a clericalist attitude infects a lay Catholic, it usually manifests itself in extreme deference to the clergy, extending the Church's authority to matters where the Church is genuinely indifferent. The success of our secular efforts should be judged by secular measures. We shouldn't seek a shortcut to success by applying an official "Catholic" label to the works of our hands. Likewise, when laypeople organize cultural activities or programs for the poor, there is no need for them to present this service as a program of the Catholic Church. They are simply serving secular society as anyone else might do.

St. Josemaría, in his life and ministry, showed that it is possible for Catholics to have both a priestly soul and a lay mentality. It is possible for both priests and laypeople. He revered the work of religious orders; and their saints, such as St. Ignatius Loyola and St. Thérèse of Lisieux, had no small influence on his spirituality. For many years his spiritual director was a Jesuit, and the founder trained the first members of Opus Dei with St. Thérèse's *Story of a Soul.* We can hear echoes of St. Ignatius's phrase "contemplatives in action" in St. Josemaría's "contemplatives in the middle of the world." We can hear echoes of St. Thérèse's "Little Way" in the founder's own emphasis on "little things." Still, by divine disposition, his ways were distinctively *not* their ways.

In fact, his ways were influenced also by his own upbringing in pre–Civil War Spain among a people divided bitterly between clericalist and anticlericalist factions. Amid such acrimony and confusion, God showed him a way that was true— and that was neither clerical nor anticlerical. It was Catholic, respecting equally the freedom and dignity proper to both ordained and laypeople. The journalist John Allen has identified St. Josemaría's way quite pointedly as "the death knell of clericalism."

Supernaturally Natural

The "secular character is proper . . . to the laity," in the words of the Second Vatican Council, and that particular character tends to produce a certain style of spirituality.

A love for the world enables laypeople to live and work with "naturalness" in any circumstance, without a distinctive dress or manner. All that should set them apart is their rectitude and their charity. If we must be set apart in some other way, let it be in the excellence of the work we do—in the service of others, as an offering to God. Secularity means behaving in a way that is consistent with our place in life, which is the very place where God has called us.

It would be unnatural for us to draw attention to ourselves with public displays of piety, just as it would be unnatural for my wife and me to draw attention to ourselves with excessive public displays of affection. My affective reserve—whether in piety or in kissing—does not mean I am ashamed of my status as a Christian or as a man married to Kimberly. Nor does it mean I am observing any kind of excessive secrecy. It is merely the reserve that's proper for the world—or at least for the particular corner of the world where I live.

In a similar way, our homes need not be decorated like medieval churches in order to be sanctified. They should be identifiably Christian, of course, but they should also be distinctively homes and not cathedrals.

Nevertheless, secularity, like any good thing, can be overdone. In our zeal to laicize our piety, we shouldn't leave people guessing whether we're Christians. That would be every bit as unnatural as wearing a monk's habit over one's work clothes. Our secularity should never lapse into secularism.

"Live as the others around you live," St. Josemaría said, "with naturalness, but 'supernaturalizing' every moment of your day."

The Bright Side

As I first made my way toward the Catholic Church, Opus Dei's sense of secularity touched me in a rather personal way. Coming from a Calvinist background, I had been taught to view the world and the fallen human race in terms of "total depravity." From such a worldview, it can seem a natural thing to hiss out the word "secular," as comedians do when they imitate televangelists, and as televangelists do when they fear the taint of the world.

But nothing could be further from the optimism I found in the Work. It is an optimism founded on secularity—and on the biblical account of God's sovereignty over creation. St. Josemaría said: "The Lord wants his children, those of us who have received the gift of faith, to proclaim the original optimistic view of creation, the love for the world which is at the heart of the Christian message."

This optimism extends even to grievous sinners, and even to those who have not accepted Jesus Christ. For they too are created by God and are as capable of conversion as we are. Against the first Protestant reformers, the Council of Trent taught that it is possible for people to do "good works" even apart from the state of grace. Pope St. Pius V condemned the Protestant notion that "all the works of nonbelievers are sins and the virtues of the [pagan] philosophers are mere vices." Without baptism, we human beings are fallen, and we need a redeemer, but we still bear God's image. Our nature is wounded by original sin, but not destroyed.

So, as Catholics, we can recognize true goodness in the works of our neighbors. We can enjoy a true appreciation of the virtues of our coworkers even if, in many other ways, they seem to be far from Christ.

This is not mere naturalism. For only grace can give saving value to human works. Only grace can turn our works into *opus Dei*. All saving good comes from the Holy Spirit, who pours grace into the hearts of God's adopted children. It is our duty to draw our friends and coworkers ever closer to Christ—ever more fully into their vocation as children of God. For God alone can endow their works with divine power.

St. Thomas Aquinas put the matter succinctly. To the question "whether without grace man can desire and accomplish what is good," he replied:

> Because human nature is not altogether corrupted
> by sin, so as to be lacking all natural good, even in
> the state of corrupted nature it can, by virtue of
> its natural endowments, achieve some particular
> good, such as building dwellings, planting vineyards
> and the like. Yet it cannot do all the good natural
> to it . . . just as a sick man can of himself make some
> movements, yet he cannot move with the movements
> of one in health, unless he is cured with the help of
> medicine.

It is our apostolate to be channels of grace for the good people we find everywhere. We recognize that they are not totally depraved. Indeed, we can recognize their virtues as virtues—and recognize when they excel us in virtue. Yet we can help them to achieve so much more. We can help them to see new horizons for themselves, for their family life, and for their work. Through our example and our friendship, we can guide them to faith, enabling them to offer their works as co-redeemers with Christ, sharing in His common priesthood.

We may not be much. But our hands may be all the boost our friends need to reach up to Jesus Christ—for He is always reaching down to them. As they are divinized by grace, their virtues will rise from the natural to the supernatural plane. It doesn't get any better than this.

The lay apostolate is a delightful apostolate, precisely because of its rich secularity. We should be happy not to hiss when we say the word, because a layman need not shy away from "passionately loving the world."

"The world awaits us. Yes, we love the world passionately because God has taught us to: *Sic Deus dilexit mundum* . . . — God so loved the world. And we love it because it is there that we fight our battles in a most beautiful war of charity, so that everyone may find the peace that Christ has come to establish."

Chapter 9

Sex and Sacrifice

You laugh because I tell you that you have a
"vocation for marriage"? Well, you have just
that: a vocation.

———THE WAY, NO. 27

At the heart of Opus Dei is the Christian experience of divine filiation. God is our Father.
We are His children in Christ Jesus, the eternal Son; thus, gathered together around His
table, the Church is the *family of God* on earth,
as the Trinity is the Family of God in heaven.

Of this mystery Pope John Paul II wrote:
"God in His deepest mystery is not a solitude,
but a family, since He has in Himself fatherhood, sonship, and the essence of the family,
which is love." Note that the pope was *not* pre-
senting the family as a metaphor for the Trinity. He did not say that God is *like* a family. He
said that God *is* a family. It would be truer to
say that human families are *like* a family than to
say that God is like a family.

All families on earth are images of divinity,
and they are domestic churches. It would be

hard to overestimate their importance in the spiritual life. Yet our families are so, well, *familiar* that it's easy to underestimate their importance.

Because priests renounce marriage, Christians sometimes speak of married life as a second-class vocation, a distraction from prayer, contemplation, and apostolate. But it's not, or at least it need not be. Once a man asked St. Josemaría, "Father, how can we make compatible dedication to our family and dedication to God?" St. Josemaría responded, "My son, you wouldn't please God if you weren't dedicated to your family. . . . There's no conflict between these two duties: they are fused together, just as the different strands of a cord, when woven together, form a rope."

Difficult Moments

In his preaching and teaching, the founder of Opus Dei constantly drew analogies between the spiritual life and family life, between institutional life (in the Church and in the Work) and home life. He spoke of the Work as simultaneously "a family and an army." He wished for both the kind of peace he knew in his childhood home.

"I speak about the sacrament of matrimony with emotion because I remember the love of my parents," he once recalled. "How well they responded at all times, and there were some quite difficult moments. They knew how to encourage one another, to bring us up in a Christian manner, and to accept the will of God with the piety God's grace inspired in them."

That there were "difficult moments" is an understatement. Josemaría was the second of six children of José and Dolores

Escrivá. Only three of those children would survive early child-hood. Josemaría himself almost died from a fever in infancy, and his mother attributed his miraculous survival to the intervention of the Blessed Virgin Mary. José was a merchant, once prosperous, who lost everything—his business and all the family's savings—because of one of his partner's questionable practices. The Escrivá family was reduced to relative poverty and humiliation.

The elder José bore it all with dignity and without bitterness. From then on, he had to work harder for less money, at lower-status jobs, and it is likely that these strains led to his early death. The Escrivá home, however, remained a haven of peace, and the parents stood united through all their troubles.

Meditating on his parents' lives of love and sacrifice, St. Josemaría developed a profound appreciation for the family in general and for the Holy Family of Nazareth in particular. His name itself is a reflection of this appreciation. He had been baptized "José María," with the names separated, but in early adulthood he began to run the names together, as "Josemaría" with no space between them, to signify the unity of Mary and Joseph—a unity he wished for every human family.

A Golden Coin

He spoke often of the joys of married life. Nevertheless, he insisted that "marriage isn't just satisfaction for the heart and senses. It's also suffering; it has two sides, like a coin."

> On the one hand, there is the joy of knowing that one is loved, the desire and enthusiasm involved in

starting a family and taking care of it, the love
of husband and wife, the happiness of seeing the
children grow up. On the other hand, there are
also sorrows and difficulties—the passing of time
that consumes the body and threatens the character
with the temptation to bitterness, the seemingly
monotonous succession of days that are apparently
always the same.

We would have a poor idea of marriage and of
human affection if we were to think that love and joy
come to an end when faced with such difficulties. It
is precisely then that our true sentiments come to
the surface. Then the tenderness of a person's gift
of himself takes root and shows itself in a true
and profound affection that is stronger than death.

As he knew from his own childhood, suffering is sometimes unavoidable. The failure of a business, the death of loved
ones—such events are impossible to predict and prepare for.
No less wearisome is the daily grind of an underemployed man,
working far below his station in life, for far less money than he
needs. Still, these are the circumstances of countless ordinary
families. To paraphrase the bumper sticker: suffering happens.
What we do with that suffering, however, is what makes us either saints or very wretched people. It's our choice, but it's not
a solitary matter. When we live in families—or in any kind of
household—our choice affects all the people around us. We either parlay our suffering into happiness for others or multiply
the misery in our homes. On trying days, the greatest sacrifice
might be to smile when we don't feel like smiling. "I've often

said," noted St. Josemaría, "that the hardest mortification can be to smile. Well, then, smile!"

"Love, my children, is sacrifice," he said. "A married man has to love his wife, and to show her that he does." Wives, for their part, "shouldn't take their husbands for granted." Affection comes naturally to a couple during courtship and engagement, but over the course of years it requires effort, even planning and preparation. He urged couples to show affection for one another throughout their years of marriage. He told them, "Never lose the refinement you had when you were engaged; if not, things don't go well." He encouraged them to try hard in little matters: what they wear, how they arrive home at the end of a long day, the care they put into the preparation of a meal, how they greet one another. The smile is the important thing; as the founder put it, Christian couples should "make sacrifices cheerfully, inconspicuously."

The Altar of the Marriage Bed

Nor did he shy away from discussion of a married couple's sexual relationship. What's more, he spoke this way at a time when many Christians avoided the topic altogether—and others discussed it only in grim terms of duty, or as a "concession to weakness." He, instead, spoke of the marriage bed as "an altar." What is placed on the altar is holy and is offered to God. Sex, like all of ordinary life, should be part of the "living sacrifice, holy and acceptable to God," of which St. Paul spoke (Romans 12:1). Our sexuality comes from God and returns to Him by way of a Christian couple's sacrificial offering—their complete gift of self, the gift of their entire lives, given to one another

and to God. St. Josemaría said, bluntly: "Sex is something noble and holy—a participation in God's creative power—which
was made for marriage."

St. Josemaría praised the pure sexual expression of married
love, and he insisted that such praise was justified—indeed,
even mandated—by Catholic doctrine: "Marriage is a sacrament that makes one flesh of two bodies. Theology expresses
this fact in a striking way when it teaches us that the matter of
the sacrament is the bodies of husband and wife. Our Lord
sanctifies and blesses the mutual love of husband and wife. He
forsees, not only a union of souls, but a union of bodies as well.
No Christian, whether or not he is called to the married state,
has a right to underestimate the value of marriage."

The sexual expression of married love is something that
sets human beings apart from animals. Truly human sex seals,
renews, and strengthens the bond of unity between a man
and a woman. The two become one, and that unity is so real
that, in nine months, they might have to give it a name. Human
beings, in other words, do not merely "mate"; they make love,
and their love makes more human beings. Thus, the Catholic
Church has always taught that sexual relations belong only in
marriage, a lifelong commitment that creates a stable home,
where children may best be welcomed. The Church has further
taught that every sexual act should respect the twofold pur-
poses of sex: the unity of the couple, and the procreation of
children.

God designed family life to draw us gradually out of ourselves, out of our selfishness, as we learn to make greater and
more loving sacrifices for the sake of others. At first each of us
lives alone, in a sense, like Adam, but it is not good to be alone.

So we enter a life with another person, through marriage. Then children, and later grandchildren, bring us ever more out of our enclosed world, to imitate God, to love like God, who gives Himself entirely and unstintingly for the sake of His children.

Children sanctify us. They bring us tremendous joys, and they demand certain hardships. They must be fed, clothed, educated, disciplined, and supervised. All of that can be costly in financial and in human terms. But we cannot choose the joys of parenting and reject the hardships. Nor can we plan a life that maximizes one while minimizing the other. Life doesn't proceed according to our plans. In the words of a popular song, life is what happens to you while you're busy making other plans.

St. Josemaría urged families to be abundantly open to new life, to cooperate with God generously. He always spoke of children as a "blessing" upon a couple. "Fear of having children? No! You must love God very much and thank Him profoundly when He sends you children. Each time a child comes into your family it's a proof of God's trust in you. Be happy. Where I come from, it's said that each child comes with a loaf of bread under its arm."

He acknowledged that this was countercultural in a time when contraceptives were routinely dispensed to newlyweds. Still, he encouraged couples to buck the trend. "Don't tolerate this infamous, anti-Christian propaganda. They want to treat you like animals! That's why I tell you to rebel, to be rebels. I am: I don't want to live like an animal. I want to live as a child of God; and you want to do likewise."

Not every act of marital union will be blessed with a resulting pregnancy, and certainly there are cases in which *natural* family planning is legitimate. All acts, however, should be open to the possibility of new life.

Nor will every marriage be blessed with children. Some couples face lifelong infertility. St. Josemaría taught them to love one another dearly and to spend their love lavishly on the people around them—to give more of their time to apostolic activity and service among their friends. This is what it means to live in the family of God. Thus, their lives, like the lives of parents, will be full.

> God, in His providence, has two ways of blessing marriages: one by giving them children; and the other, sometimes, because He loves them so much, by not giving them children. I don't know which is the better blessing. In any event, let each one accept his own.
>
> To those couples who don't have children, I tell you to love each other very much, very much. Human love within marriage is most pleasing to God. Love one another with all your soul, according to the natural law and God's law."

A still more generous gift of human sexuality is celibacy for the sake of God's kingdom. Celibacy gives men and women greater freedom to serve God in a variety of different circumstances, with maximum mobility. A celibate life, moreover, anticipates the glorious fulfillment of life in Christ at the end of time. "For when they rise from the dead, they neither marry nor are given in marriage, but are like angels in heaven" (Mark 12:25). A good many members of Opus Dei have accepted this call. It came from God, but they heard it from St. Josemaría: "Many live like angels in the middle of the world. You . . . why not you?"

Thinking with Mother

As I said earlier, St. Josemaría applied the family paradigm to life in Opus Dei and also to life in the Church. This is yet another quality that made Opus Dei attractive to me as a new Catholic. Members tended not to divide the Church along left-right, liberal-conservative, or any other factional lines. They saw the Church as a family whose essential unity trumped all differences of opinion, taste, and preference. Members of Opus Dei seemed to me to find it easy to "think with the Church" because they thought of the Church as a family rather than an institution or an ideology. For St. Josemaría, the Catholic Church was "Mother Church," feeding her young with her own substance in the Eucharist, training her young for life with good doctrine.

What the faithful of Opus Dei had, they wanted to share. It was the timeless truth of Christianity. But it was more than that: it was membership in a family, life as a child of God in the household of God. And so their apostolate always had a catechetical content and always had a charitable style, respecting the true freedom of God's children, but gently reproving and correcting whenever necessary.

By the time of my life when I met these good people, I was already a husband and father. God was drawing me outside myself and showing me new horizons.

For me, from the beginning, Opus Dei felt like home.

Chapter 10

The Workshop of Nazareth: On Unity of Life

Calmness. Peace. Intense life within you. Without
that wild hurry, without that frenzy for change,
you can work from your proper place in life. And,
like a powerful generator of spiritual electricity,
you will give light and energy to very many,
without losing your own vigor and light.

—THE WAY, NO. 837

Members of Opus Dei keep a lively devotion
to St. Joseph, which they learned from St.
Josemaría. Every day, as the founder began his
period of mental prayer, he asked the help of
Jesus's foster-father, addressing him as "my father and lord." Every year, on the feast of St.
Joseph, March 19, the faithful of the prelature
who have already made the "oblation" renew
their vocational commitment.

Devotion to St. Joseph is an amazing and
recurring phenomenon in history. The great
patriarch gave us not a word to go on in Sacred
Scripture. He moves silently through the pages
of two gospels, always open to the promptings

of angels, ever mindful of the safety of his wife and Child. In the other gospels, he appears only briefly, in the descriptions of Jesus as "the carpenter's son."

He was definitely the strong, silent type. And how strong he must have been—strong in faith, in body, and in fatherly virtue—to bring his family safely to Egypt and then back to Nazareth, when all the powers of Herod and of hell were arrayed against them.

If all that St. Josemaría taught us was devotion to St. Joseph, he would have taught us much. For in the life of St. Joseph we see all the essential elements of Opus Dei. We see fatherhood and sonship. We glimpse a happy family life, amid many difficulties. We see an active piety. We meet a man who works hard and is known for his work. And all of these various elements are united in his life. St. Joseph lived his life at peace because he did not allow himself to be pulled in many directions. He lived well the quality that St. Josemaría called "unity of life."

At Home with the Word

It can be instructive for us to imagine the household of the Holy Family—not just their family life but their physical environment too. Their house was probably a typical residence of its time: a small structure of stone or wood, a single room lit by a single lamp and ventilated by a single doorway. We know from Luke's gospel that the Holy Family was poor; at Jesus's presentation, they made the sacrifice designated for poor families, "a pair of turtledoves, or two young pigeons" (Luke 2:24). Yet we may assume that, since St. Joseph was a craftsman, their house was better constructed than most, if modest in size.

The lone room in the house was probably sparsely furnished, as it had to be a dining room by day and a bedroom by night. It might have served as the workshop for the family business as well. The family bed was a mat (or mats) on the floor, and in colder seasons some families shared their sleeping space with their livestock, if they owned any.

There was no clear dividing line between the nuclear family and their neighbors. Even in the north country, in Galilee of the Gentiles, villages were often tribal settlements. So everyone in a peasant's limited world was "family." There was, in fact, no distinct word for "cousin"; all blood relatives were considered "brothers and sisters," regardless of their degree of relation. What's more, an individual's family ties extended further still, to all the members of the twelve tribes of Israel, or at least the remnant then dwelling in the ancestral lands.

One's village, to a certain degree, defined the horizons of one's world. Long travel was difficult and somewhat dangerous, because bandits and predatory animals prowled the roads by night. When villagers traveled to Jerusalem, as they did for pilgrimage on the great holy days, they traveled with their tribe all around them—not with strangers, as we often travel today. And the caravan might be very large—so large, so safe, and so familiar that a child could disappear for a day before his parents began to worry (see Luke 2:42–45).

The pilgrimages marked high points of the religious calendar of the Jews. But it can be misleading to speak of the "religious calendar," because for God's chosen people there was only one calendar, and it was suffused with the law and the liturgy of the covenant. The liturgy was not merely the ceremonies that went on at the faraway temple, or the rites observed at the twice-weekly synagogue assemblies; the liturgy was what permeated all of life. Israel's law ensured that every day began with an invocation of the Almighty and every meal was a sacred event begun with a blessing.

Such was the life of St. Joseph, an ordinary laborer of the tribe of Judah in a province of a far-flung empire. It was, in many ways, different from your life and mine. But it was a life of prayer, work, family, joy, and suffering, and it was a perfectly integrated life. St. Joseph gave St. Josemaría a model of "unity of life," and he can give it to all of us too.

This model is a challenge for modern people in secularist societies. Our culture conditions us to make time for religion, but to segregate that time. We might plug it into our Franklin Planner or our Blackberry so that our Sunday mornings are inviolable and sacred. But where is God in all the rest of our week? Where is God when we work and play and rest and help our children with their algebra?

St. Josemaría saw that the great modern temptation for Christians was "to lead a kind of double life: on the one hand, an inner life, a life related to God; and on the other, as something separate and distinct, their professional, social and family lives, made up of small earthly realities." But he insisted that we must not give in to the temptation: "There is only one life, made of flesh and spirit. And it is that life which has to become, in both body and soul, holy and filled with God: we discover the invisible God in the most visible and material things."

The life that St. Josemaría proposed is an integrated life, like St. Joseph's—wholly secular yet holy too, immersed in the bustle of the village (whether Galilean or global) but always immersed in God as well. It is a life that unites the divine and the human, the theoretical and the practical, the professional and the familial. It is a life directed toward heaven, yet, in a certain sense, already there.

It makes for happy days, even amid difficulties, and it accounts for the joy I found in those first members of Opus Dei I met. "Our Lord does not expect us to be unhappy in our life on earth and await a reward only in the next life," St. Josemaría preached.

> God wants us to be happy on earth too, but with a desire for the other, total happiness that only He can give. In this life, the contemplation of supernatural reality, the action of grace in our souls, our love for our neighbor as a result of our love for God—all these are already a foretaste of heaven, a beginning that is destined to grow from day to day. We Christians cannot resign ourselves to leading a double life. Our life must be a strong and simple unity into which all our actions converge.

Divine filiation is the unifying principle. St. Joseph learned how to be a son of God by watching the Son of God grow up in his midst. Jesus was the only truly adorable little child, and surely His foster-father adored Him, learning from a Child how to trust His Father and abandon Himself to His will. We too can learn from small children, and indeed we must. Jesus Himself informed us: "Truly, I say to you, unless you turn and become like children, you will never enter the kingdom of heaven" (Matthew 18:3).

Little children do not live divided lives. They may play different roles in different games from hour to hour, but they remain themselves, at ease in their parents' home, their parents' world. When we learn from them, our life of spiritual childhood brings unity to life.

The spiritual life of Opus Dei is rich in devotional customs. I've heard its spirituality described as "Trinitarian," "eucharistic," "christocentric," and "Marian." It is all of those things—with a healthy dose of angelology thrown in—and it can be all those things because it all boils down to divine filiation, a life of childhood. "This unity of life built on the presence of God our Father, can and ought to be a daily reality," in the words of the founder.

The presence of God is key. God is always with us, whether we acknowledge Him or not. He is always watching, wise and willing to help us if only we ask. That act of awareness and that act of asking—those mark the difference between work that is *ours* and work that is *God's,* between *opus noster* and *opus Dei.* Our work might make the hours pass by, but God's work makes the kingdom come. The latter is a far more fulfilling way to spend one's life.

The plan of life that St. Josemaría left to the Church, the spirituality he conveyed, is emblematic of his role as a "sower of peace and love." Where there is unity in life, there is no division, and so there is far less inner conflict and far more inner serenity. "To work in this way is to pray. To study thus is likewise prayer. Research done with this spirit is prayer too. We are always doing the same thing, for everything can be prayer, all activity can and should lead us to God, nourish our intimate dealings with Him, from morning to night. Any honorable work can be prayer and all prayerful work is apostolate. In this way the soul develops a unity of life, which is both simple and strong."

Home Is Where the Heart Goes

We are children of God in the eternal Son of God, who is also the Son of Mary. We are at home in the Trinity, at home in the Mass. But we are at home also in the workshop, as Joseph was in the workshop of Nazareth. And of course, we are at home when we're at home.

It is one life, spent at one with God, at one with His Church, and at one with all His children. "Jesus does not allow any division here: 'No one can serve two masters, for he will either hate the one and love the other, or if he subjects himself to the first, he will despise the other.' The exclusive choice of God that a Christian makes when he responds fully to his call, impels him to refer everything to Our Lord and, at the same time, to give his neighbor everything that justice requires."

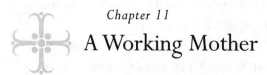

Chapter 11
A Working Mother

But . . . have you never seen the mothers of this
earth, with arms outstretched, following their
little ones when, without anyone's help, they
venture to take their first shaky steps? You are not
alone: Mary is close beside you.

—THE WAY, NO. 900

A father builds a house, but a mother makes a home.

Priests of Opus Dei, following the example of St. Josemaría, tend to close their meditations and their homilies by invoking the Blessed Mother. A Marian garland trims the entire plan of life, with daily Rosary and Angelus, weekly antiphons, and annual pilgrimages. All the faithful of the Work, and many who follow its spirituality, end their prayers with the aspiration: "Holy Mary, our hope, seat of wisdom, pray for us!" or, "Holy Mary, our hope, handmaid of the Lord, pray for us!"

In calling us His children, God has given us His life, holding nothing back. Whatever He has given to His only begotten Son, He gives now to the "assembly of the firstborn" (Hebrews 12:23).

As members of His family, we are "heirs of God and co-heirs with Christ" (Romans 8:17), and so we share in everything that is Christ's. We share His household, the Church (see Ephesians 2:19–20). We share His name, in which we are baptized (see Matthew 28:18–20). We sit at His table (1 Corinthians 10:21). We share His very flesh and blood (Hebrews 2:14).

And we share His mother. Mary is the Mother of the God who came to earth to be our Brother. She is Mother of God, and our mother too.

God has brought us into His household, His family, and families normally have mothers. Not all families have mothers, of course, but those who have lost their mother feel the absence.

The "code" of Opus Dei is no secret. Nor is it obscure or arcane. It is divine filiation. We are children—children of God. And because we are children of God, we are children of Mary.

St. Josemaría gave her the honor she is due as mother in his little family, the Work. For as much as St. Joseph—and more because God preserved her from sin—she is an image, an icon of the love, sacrifice, and communion of Opus Dei.

> Our mother is a model of correspondence to grace.
> If we contemplate her life, Our Lord will give us the
> light we need to divinize our everyday existence. . . .
> First, let us imitate her love. Charity cannot be
> content with just nice feelings; it must find its way
> into our conversations and, above all, into our deeds.
> The Virgin did not merely pronounce her fiat; in

every moment she fulfilled that firm and irrevocable decision. So should we. When God's love gets through to us and we come to know what he desires, we ought to commit ourselves to be faithful, loyal—and then be so in fact. Because "not everyone who says to Me, Lord, Lord, will enter the kingdom of heaven, but he who does the will of My Father in heaven."

We must imitate her natural and supernatural refinement. She is a privileged creature in the history of salvation, for in Mary "the Word became flesh and dwelled among us." But she is a reserved, quiet witness. She never wished to be praised, for she never sought her own glory. Mary is present at the mysteries surrounding the infancy of her Son, but these are "normal" mysteries, so to speak. When the great miracles take place and the crowds acclaim them in amazement, she is nowhere to be found. In Jerusalem when Christ, riding a little donkey, is proclaimed king, we don't catch a glimpse of Mary. But after all have fled, she reappears next to the cross. This way of acting bespeaks personal greatness and depth, the sanctity of her soul.

Following her example of obedience to God, we can learn to serve delicately without being slavish. In Mary we don't find the slightest trace of the attitude of the foolish virgins, who obey, but thoughtlessly. Our Lady listens attentively to what God wants, ponders what she doesn't fully understand and asks about what she doesn't know. Then she gives herself completely to doing the divine will: "Behold the handmaid of the Lord, be it done unto me according to your word." Isn't that marvelous? The blessed Virgin, our teacher in all we do, shows us here that obedience to God is not servile, does not bypass our conscience. We should be inwardly moved to discover the "freedom of the children of God."

Chapter 12

Turn Up the Romance

If Love, even human love, gives so much
consolation here, what will Love not be in heaven?

——THE WAY, NO. 428

I still remember the moment when I "got" Opus Dei. Up till then, I had admired its fidelity to Christian doctrine, its plan of life, and the kindness and intelligence of its people. But I didn't truly understand what set Opus Dei apart from anything else.

As I look back, I see that I had good excuses for my incomprehension. For one, I was new to the Catholic faith. I was also distracted—to the point of anxiety. My newfound faith was placing a strain on my marriage; any time I might have spent studying the spirit of Opus Dei, I was instead spending to prepare my explanations of all the distinctive Catholic beliefs and practices. "Always be prepared," said St. Peter, "to make a defense to anyone who calls you to account" (1 Peter 3:15). I figured that went double if one's own wife was doing the calling.

Kimberly was (and still is) a very articulate, very well educated, very devout and ardent daughter of a Presbyterian minister. She holds a master's degree from one of the most
respected evangelical theological schools in America. She knew
what she believed, and she knew why. As an intelligent and informed Calvinist, she knew why she was Protestant. The very
stuff of the *Protest*ant Reformation was a *protest* against certain
traditional Catholic doctrines and devotions. Kimberly had
very serious objections to Catholicism, at least as she perceived
it. She worried that my turning toward Marian devotion was a
turning away from Jesus Christ. She worried that my use of
sacramentals might be superstitious—and that my invocation
of the saints might be idolatrous.

So I did what any rationalist would do in such a situation. I
spent hours of every day carefully researching and crafting answers to her objections, constructing arguments out of those
answers, and then mentally rehearsing the best ways to present
those arguments.

I was genuinely surprised when my strategy didn't seem to
work. Kimberly and I would stay up till three debating doctrinal differences and then continue the conversation at breakfast
in the morning. Yet the more irrefutable my arguments, the
more I seemed to push her away—and not only from the
Catholic Church but from me as well. After a while, she refused to read the articles and books I recommended for her
reading. She refused to read even a paragraph of a particular article about the Blessed Virgin Mary. I could tell that she was beginning to dread the start of our conversations for fear of
where they might end up.

I was frustrated and heartbroken. I turned to a friend of

mine, Gil, who happened to be a member of Opus Dei. In painful detail I explained how much I had tried to anticipate Kimberly's concerns and how carefully I had tried to address every one of them.

I saw Gil wince.

"What?" I asked him. "What's wrong?"

He looked at me in the most brotherly way and said, "Why don't you turn down the apologetics and turn up the romance?"

At first I was skeptical. But then I took the problem to my confessor, an Opus Dei priest, who gave me strikingly similar counsel. The message couldn't be clearer: "Lighten up on the theology, Scott. Go heavy on the affection."

It hardly seemed right to me. Here I was, a theologian advised to abandon the queen of sciences, the most noble pursuit I knew—all for the sake of what? Candlelight and sweet nothings?

But now lightning had struck twice in the same place in my heart, and the bolts flashed from two men whom I respected deeply. I would give it a try.

I tried at first to rediscover the common ground of our marriage, to focus on what united us as a couple rather than what divided us. I began to realize how seldom, for example, I had initiated conversations about our children, who were then very small. We began, again, to laugh together and to appreciate the small daily discoveries of young parents.

Eventually, we were able to pray together once again, without contention or provocation.

It was working. Instead of trying to build the perfect argument, I was trying to be a better husband to my wife, a better father to my children, a better son to my parents and my in-laws.

The effect on our marriage was electric. I'll spare you the details. I will only point out that the day arrived when Kimberly began to ask me questions about the Catholic faith. And it wasn't long before she too was asking to be received into full communion with the Church.

"Turning up the romance" accomplished what endless debate could never force.

And that, to me, is Opus Dei.

So much of the spirit of Opus Dei was wrapped up in that simple advice: "Turn up the romance." What was Gil telling me, underneath it all?

He was telling me to respect Kimberly's freedom. (That's Opus Dei.)

He was telling me that grace builds on nature. (That's Opus Dei.)

He was nudging me toward secularity and away from an annoyingly clericalist approach to the problem. (That's Opus Dei.)

And he was emphasizing the importance (and even the sexiness) of ordinary family life. (And that's Opus Dei.)

These are all consequences of the truth at the heart of Opus Dei: divine filiation. What Gil led me to see was that all creation awaited the revelation of God's children and the glorious freedom of the children of God (see Romans 8:19–21)—but that God would do the revealing, and in His good time. It was my job to be faithful to my marriage covenant in ways I had too long been neglecting.

When I could bring myself to trust in Kimberly's conversion as God's work, not mine, I could more truly love Kimberly, and in ways that even she could recognize.

Loving Like Jacob

This unexpected success at home caused a ripple effect throughout my life. I found myself applying Gil's principles to my professional labors and prayer. It's not that I started seeking romantic encounters on the job. Rather, I "turned up the romance" in my overall spiritual life.

A biblical illustration might be in order. Consider the story of Jacob, in the Book of Genesis (Genesis 29). One day while traveling, the young man met a woman "beautiful and lovely" named Rachel. He was so smitten that he wept aloud. Soon he approached Rachel's father, Laban, and asked for the privilege of marrying her. So much did he love her that he promised to work in Laban's lands for seven years in order to merit such a wife. "So Jacob served seven years for Rachel, and they seemed to him but a few days because of the love he had for her" (v. 20). Jacob would, in fact, labor another seven years that way, because of the trickery of Laban.

Notice, however, that Jacob did not toil in bitterness. Nor did he grimly ponder all the places he'd rather be than pushing sheep through the pastures of an untrustworthy man. He worked with joy because his heart was set on the goal: the love of Rachel. He kept a spirit of service because he was serving the only man who could lead him to that goal. In fact, when all was said and done and Jacob had married Rachel, he served Laban for another seven years, out of gratitude!

We all have so much to learn. I am no longer speaking here

about domestic bliss. I'm talking about something far greater: our goal of reaching heaven.

For that goal, how much should we be willing to work? Seven years? Fourteen? Twenty-one? Seventy? The longest lifetime would not be enough.

And how much joy should brim our hearts when we are working for the love of God? How much love and loyalty should we bear toward the boss and our coworkers?

There is not a hint of tin-can mysticism in Jacob. He doesn't daydream about the delights of a remote retirement. For love's sake, he applies elbow grease, one hour after another hour, and then another hour after yet another, till seven years have passed and it seems to him but a few days.

Opus Dei taught me to strive after the kind of love that Jacob lived, to keep the sense of adventure in marriage and in everyday life, to remain mindful of the high stakes of ordinary conversations, to recognize the everlasting consequences of lingering glances—especially when they're directed heavenward.

All this is true in the orders of grace and nature. The Work of God is to work with love and joy, daily turning up the romance in our ordinary life. For God awaits our tender love, wherever we are and at every moment.

From such romance good homes are made, in the Church and in the world.

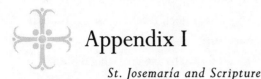

Appendix I

St. Josemaría and Scripture

The following article appeared in *Romana: The Bulletin of the Prelature of the Holy Cross and Opus Dei* 35 (July–December 2002): 382ff.

PASSIONATELY LOVING THE WORD: THE USE OF SACRED
SCRIPTURE IN THE WRITINGS OF SAINT JOSEMARÍA
By Scott Hahn

The world knows Josemaría Escrivá (1902–75) best as the founder of Opus Dei and the Priestly Society of the Holy Cross. Members of the Catholic Church know him best for his personal holiness and intercessory power, and so, on October 6, 2002, Pope John Paul II canonized Josemaría Escrivá, declaring him worthy all over the world of public veneration and imitation.

In a certain sense we can fully understand the accomplishments of St. Josemaría, or the graces he received, when we come to understand his use of the Scriptures. For, in Opus Dei, he worked out a thoroughly biblical spirituality; and he himself saw the institution as built on solidly scriptural foundations. In perhaps the most powerful précis of his spirituality, the homily "Passionately Loving the World," St. Josemaría repeatedly claims the Bible as his primary witness: "This doctrine of Sacred

Scripture, as you know, is to be found in the very core of the spirit of Opus Dei." "This I have been teaching all the time, using words from Holy Scripture."

Indeed, I would go so far as to say that the Bible always served as St. Josemaría's primary referential language. Though he was steeped in the teachings of the Fathers and Doctors of the Church, though he was fluent in scholastic theology, and though he kept current with trends in contemporary theology, it was to Scripture that he returned again and again in his preaching and writing, and it was to Scripture that he directed his spiritual children in Opus Dei.

He saw clearly the unity of the two testaments, the Old and the New. The Old Testament oracles did not lose relevance for St. Josemaría just because they had been fulfilled in the New. Rather, they shone with a new and more brilliant light. He did not hesitate to hold up the patriarchs and prophets of Israel as spiritual exemplars for Christians today:

> When you receive Our Lord in the Holy Eucharist, thank Him from the bottom of your heart for being so good as to be with you.
>
> Have you ever stopped to consider that it took centuries and centuries before the Messiah came? All those patriarchs and prophets praying together with the whole people of Israel: Come, Lord, the land is parched!
>
> If only your loving expectation were like this.

He quoted frequently from both the Old and New Testaments, but especially from the Gospels, to which Tradition has assigned a preeminent place. Perhaps no phrases appear so often in his writings and homilies as those that invoke the sacred page: "as the Gospel tells us . . ."; "as the Gospel advises . . ."; "Sacred Scripture tells us . . ."; "the Gospels relate . . ."; "Remember the Gospel story. . . ."

According to Bishop Álvaro del Portillo, who was St. Josemaría's most loyal son, confessor, and successor in the direction of Opus Dei: "I was myself always impressed with the facility with which he could cite from memory exact phrases from the Holy Bible. Even during everyday conversations, he would often take a starting point from some pertinent text in order to inspire us to a more profound prayer. He lived on the word of God."

Scripture as a Measure

The founding of Opus Dei took place on October 2, 1928, when St. Josemaría "saw" the Work of God (as yet unnamed) as a way of sanctification in daily work and in the fulfillment of the Christian's ordinary duties.

What did Opus Dei look like at that moment? We do not know the visual details, but we can glimpse the Work incarnate in the later writings of the founder. There, he spoke of the Scriptures as a reliable measure of his way of life, which was "as old as the Gospel but, like the Gospel, ever new." At the beginning of his seminal work, *The Way,* he wrote: "How I wish your bearing and conversation were such that, on seeing or hearing you, people would say: This man reads the life of Jesus Christ." Conversely, in discussing those who do not live Christian charity, St. Josemaría said, "They seem not to have read the Gospel."

His own reading of the Gospel and of Scripture in general was illuminated by his particular foundational charism, which led him to develop ideas that had been passed over in previous theology. He is notable for his novel or renewed emphasis on certain notions found in the Scriptures: the universal call to holiness, for example, and the sanctification of ordinary life. Again and again, he was drawn to contemplate the Gospel's tantalizing allusions of Jesus's thirty years of hidden life. Even in these relative silences he found a model for the "hidden life" of ordinary people working in the world.

Study of the Scripture, then, was essential to his personal spirituality and to the program he developed for members of Opus Dei. He assumed that Scripture not only enabled readers to know Jesus but also empowered them to imitate him. "In our own life we must reproduce Christ's life. We need to come to know him by reading and meditating on Scripture."

His Method

St. Josemaría practiced and preached a particular way to approach the Scriptures in prayer. His way is intensive rather than exhaustive. Bishop del Portillo recalled that the founder "gave constant proof of an extraordinary veneration for Sacred Scripture. The Holy Bible, together with the tradition of the Church, was the source from which he ceaselessly drew for his personal prayer and preaching. Every day he read some pages—about a chapter—of Scripture, generally from the New Testament."

This practice of daily study of the New Testament—about five minutes' time—St. Josemaría prescribed to all those whom he directed. He urged them, when they read, to enter imaginatively into the biblical scenes, assuming the role of one of the characters or a bystander. "I advised you to read the New Testament and to enter into each scene and take part in it, as one more of the characters. The minutes you spend in this way each day enable you to incarnate the Gospel, reflect it in your life and help others to reflect it."

Elsewhere, he developed the idea further, again emphasizing the imaginative effort as an almost sensory experience:

> Make it a habit to mingle with the characters who
> appear in the New Testament. Capture the flavor
> of those moving scenes where the Master performs
> works that are both divine and human, and tells us,
> with human and divine touches, the wonderful story
> of his pardon for us and his enduring Love for his
> children. Those foretastes of Heaven are renewed
> today, for the Gospel is always true: we can feel,
> we can sense, we can even say we touch God's
> protection with our own hands.

The Power to Transform

Though his actual reading took only five minutes per day, we must not confine St. Josemaría's meditation on Scripture to those few moments. He also prayed the Scriptures in his daily Mass and in his recitation of the Divine Office. He frequently used biblical commentaries of the Fathers of the Church for spiritual reading. Indeed, he insisted that a Christian's personal meditation on Scripture must feed his mental prayer as well as the spontaneous prayer that fills his entire day. "For we do need to know it well, to have it in our heart and mind, so that at any time, without any book, we can close our eyes and contemplate [Christ's] life, watching it like a movie. In this way the words and actions of Our Lord will come to mind in all the different circumstances of our life."

With the reading of Scripture, then, comes the grace of transformation, of conversion. Reading the Bible is not a passive act, but an active seeking and finding. "If we do this without holding back, Christ's words will enter deep into our soul and will really change us. For 'the word of God is living and active, sharper than any two-edged sword, piercing to the division of the soul and spirit, of joints and marrow, and discerning the thoughts and intentions of the heart' (Hebrews 4:12)."

Divine Filiation and the Revealed Word

At the heart of Opus Dei is a single idea. Said St. Josemaría: "Divine filiation is the basis of the spirit of Opus Dei. All men are children of God." St. Josemaría experienced his own divine sonship mystically, one day in 1931, while riding a streetcar in Madrid. At that moment, he felt "in an explicit, clear, definitive way, the reality" of being a child of God, and he left the streetcar babbling, "*Abba, Pater! Abba, Pater!*" (cf. Galatians 4:6).

That experience had a profound influence on his subsequent thinking, preaching, writing, and prayer. All Christian doctrine, he believed, can and should be considered in light of this truth. But we find a most powerful example of God's fatherly care when we contemplate that Salvation history is the story of God's fatherly plan for bestowing divine sonship on all men.

Many Fathers of the Church, most notably St. John Chrysostom, spoke of God's revelation in terms of "accommodation" and "condescension," which Chrysostom understood as fatherly actions. In order to reveal Himself, God *accommodates* Himself to man, just as a human father stoops down to look his children in the eye. As a human father will sometimes resort to "baby talk," God sometimes communicates by condescension— that is, He speaks as humans would speak, in the language of humans, as if He had the same passions and weaknesses. Thus, in Scripture, we read of God "repenting" His decisions, when surely God is never in need of repentance.

Yet human fathers do not only stoop down to their children's level. They also raise their children up to function on an adult level. In a similar way, God also, at times, communicates by elevation—that is, He lifts his children up to a divine level, endowing merely human words with divine power (as in the case of the prophets).

Relying on God's fatherly care, St. Josemaría trusted the word of Scripture as he would trust the words of his father. His filial confidence is exemplary of the timeless Christian belief that "the books of both the Old and New Testaments *in their entirety, with all their parts,* are sacred and canonical because written under the inspiration of the Holy Spirit, they have God as their author. . . . Therefore, since everything asserted by the inspired authors or sacred writers must be held to be asserted by the Holy Spirit, it follows that the books of Scripture must be acknowledged as teaching solidly, faithfully, and without error that truth which God wanted put into sacred writings for the sake of salvation."

Bishop del Portillo recalled that St. Josemaría exuded confidence in the divine origin of the holy Scriptures, not only when he preached and wrote, but also in his everyday conversation. "One sign of his reverence for Sacred Scriptures was his habit of introducing his quotations with the words 'The Holy Spirit says. . . .' It was not just a manner of speaking; it was a heartfelt act of faith which helped us really feel the eternal validity of, and the solid weight of truth behind, expressions which might otherwise have sounded overly familiar."

Literal and Spiritual Senses

St. Josemaría placed tremendous emphasis on the imaginative assimilation of small details of the Gospel narratives. No word was superfluous for him; no detail so small as to lack significance. In his view, the Holy Spirit did not waste words.

Yet his care for the literal-historical sense did not render him blind to the Scripture's "spiritual sense." For the Church has traditionally interpreted the biblical texts as both *literally* true and as *spiritual* signs of Christ, of heaven, or of moral truths. Indeed, though St. Josemaría never himself employed the terminology of "literal exegesis" or "spiritual exegesis," he stands as one of the great spiritual exegetes of his time. I agree with Cardinal Parente, who observed that St. Josemaría's commentaries on Sacred Scripture reflected a "profundity and immediacy often superior even to that found in the works of the Fathers of the Church."

Here, I could multiply examples. Consider this compact teaching from *The Way:* "Like the good sons of Noah, throw the mantle of charity over the defects you see in your father, the Priest" (no. 75). St. Josemaría evokes the scene of Noah's shameful drunkenness (Genesis 9:20–23) and draws out a stunning moral teaching for contemporary life in the Church. This is spiritual exegesis at its most concise and incisive. In a single line, we learn from our Old Testament ancestors why we should never spread scandal about the clergy, whom in faith we call "Father."

We see another striking example of the founder's spiritual exegesis when he compares the sins of Christians to the biblical Esau's willingness to exchange his birthright for a bowl of lentils (Genesis 25:29–34). For a moment's pleasure, such Christians are willing to alienate themselves from God and even forsake heaven altogether.

St. Josemaría did not hesitate to actualize the biblical text by applying it to contemporary life, and here he stands in the line of great exegetes from Sts. Augustine and John Chrysostom to St. Anthony of Padua and Jacques Bossuet. Scholars call this extensive interpretation the "accommodated spiritual sense."

Still, none of these spiritual insights supersedes the literal-historical truth of the biblical text, which St. Josemaría revered. In the words of St. Thomas Aquinas, "All other senses of Sacred Scripture are based on the literal."

Thus, to lay a firm foundation, St. Josemaría made careful studies of what biblical science had to say about the cultural milieu of ancient Israel and the Roman empire in the time of Jesus. His preaching on Christ's passion, for example, shows that he was familiar with historical scholarship on Roman methods of crucifixion. His homilies on St. Joseph display a keen interest not only in philology, but also in the customs of ancient Jewish family life and labor.

Occasionally, St. Josemaría received extraordinary, divine illuminations revealing a particular spiritual sense of a biblical text. He reported that, on the feast of the Transfiguration in 1931, while saying Mass:

> when I raised the host there was *another* voice,
> without the sound of speech. A voice, perfectly clear
> as always, said, *Et ego, si exaltatus fuero a terra, omnia*
> *traham ad me ipsum!* ["And I, when I am lifted up from
> the earth, will draw all things to Myself"; 1 John
> 12:32]. And here is what I mean by this: I am not
> saying it in the sense in which it is said in Scripture.
> I say it to you meaning that you should put me at
> the pinnacle of all human activities, so that in every
> place in the world there will be Christians with a
> dedication that is personal and totally free—
> Christians who will be other Christs.

This sudden insight had a profound influence on the subsequent development of Opus Dei. Surely, it came from God. But here as always, grace builds on nature and perfects it. What St. Josemaría describes is clearly an instance of infused contemplation—but one that is firmly based on a sustained and disciplined *life* of biblical meditation.

I can think of few anecdotes that so perfectly illustrate a principle sketched out by the Pontifical Biblical Commission in its 1993 document *The Interpretation of the Bible in the Church:* "It is above all through the liturgy that Christians come into contact with Scripture. . . . In principle, the liturgy, and especially the sacramental liturgy, the high point of which is the eucharistic celebration, brings about the most perfect actualization of the biblical texts. . . . Christ is then 'present in his word, because it is he himself who speaks when sacred Scripture is read in the Church' *(Sacrosanctum concilium, 7)*. Written text thus becomes living word."

Text and Context

St. Josemaría studied the Scriptures earnestly. He knew, however, that the Bible was not a self-evident or self-interpreting text. And, though God sometimes gave him supernatural lights, the founder knew that these were extraordinary phenomena—certainly not the usual way of coming to understand a text.

If he could not rely on his own lights, nor depend exclusively on mystical phenomena, where did he habitually turn in the ordinary course of his biblical studies? He looked to the Church and her living tradition, to which the ancient Fathers are "always timely witnesses." A cursory glance at any volume of his homilies will reveal his intimate familiarity with the works of St. Jerome, St. Basil, St. Augustine, St. Thomas Aquinas.

St. Josemaría tested all his scriptural insights—even those he believed to be divinely inspired—against the witness of the Fathers and the papal and conciliar magisterium. For he well knew the dangers that lurked in an overreliance on private interpretation of the Scriptures. Indeed, he found a clear warning on the matter—in the pages of the Scriptures! On the first Sunday of Lent 1952, he reflected on the subtle ways Satan tempted Jesus in the desert:

It's worth thinking about the method Satan uses with Our Lord Jesus Christ: he argues with texts from the sacred books, twisting and distorting their meaning in a blasphemous way. Jesus doesn't let himself be deceived: the Word made flesh knows well the divine word, written for the salvation of men—not their confusion and downfall.

So, we can conclude that anyone who is united to Jesus Christ through Love will never be deceived by manipulation of the holy Scripture, for he knows that it is typical of the devil to try to confuse the Christian conscience, juggling with the very words of eternal wisdom, trying to turn light into darkness.

We may conclude from the current Babel of conflicting biblical interpretations that Satan's methods have not changed much over the millennia. Amid such confusion, St. Josemaría stands out as a model of intelligent yet childlike faith. While many Christian exegetes spent the twentieth century retreating into agnosticism and irrelevance, St. Josemaría thrived on a complete and critically informed confidence in the Bible and in the Church as its infallible interpreter.

We can see, touch, and study his legacy in the Navarre Bible project, which he inspired. Initiated in the early 1970s at the University of Navarre in Spain, the Navarre Bible offers a reliable and beautiful translation of the Scriptures, supplemented by ample quotations from the Church councils, Fathers, and Doctors. This project has done much to enable non-theologians and non-ecclesiastics to enjoy the Bible as St. Josemaría did, and to be enriched by it as he was.

The Place of the Bible

St. Josemaría's most profound encounters with Sacred Scripture came not in his study or even in his oratory pew, but in the liturgy. Like the Fathers of the Second Vatican Council, he saw the Mass as the encounter *par excellence* with Jesus Christ in "bread and word." The Holy Mass, within which is found the Liturgy of the Word, is, for St. Josemaría, the "root and center" of interior life.

His homilies—which are saturated with quotations and allusions from both testaments of the Bible—always find their focus in the liturgical season, and specifically in the readings of the day. Indeed, he saw the Mass as the supernatural habitat of his homilies:

> You have just been listening to the solemn reading of
> the two texts of Sacred Scripture for the Mass of the
> twenty-first Sunday after Pentecost. Having heard the
> Word of God you are already in the right atmosphere
> for the words I want to address to you: words of a
> priest, spoken to a large family of the children of
> God in his Holy Church. Words, therefore, which
> are intended to be supernatural, proclaiming the
> greatness of God and his mercies towards men;
> words to prepare you for today's great celebration
> of the Eucharist.

Like the Fathers of the Church and the Fathers of the Second Vatican Council, St. Josemaría looked upon the Mass as a particularly graced moment for receiving the Word of God.

The inspirations received in the Liturgy of the Word should be profound and lasting: "We now listen to the word of Scripture, the epistle and the Gospel—light from the Holy Spirit, who speaks through human voices so as to make our intellect come to know and contemplate, to strengthen our will and make our desire for action effective."

The Virtuous Interpreter

In canonizing Josemaría Escrivá, the Church has held him up as worthy of imitation. There can be no doubt that such imitation must include intensive study of the Scriptures, meditative reading of the Scriptures, and disciplined prayer of the Scriptures. His own daily program witnessed to this. The "norms of piety" he followed—and which he bequeathed to his children in Opus Dei—are saturated in biblical quotations.

What is clearly central for him, however, is the encounter with Jesus Christ, the identification with Jesus Christ, to the point of becoming *"ipse Christus,"* Christ himself. This goal must be attained through certain determinate means, among them the meditative reading of the Gospels. Thus, one cannot understand or live the vocation to Opus Dei without at least aspiring to a high degree of biblical fluency.

Though he lived most of his life before the Second Vatican Council, St. Josemaría anticipated much of its teaching—certainly, at least, its emphasis on the universal call to holiness and apostolate, which had been a hallmark of Opus Dei since 1928. I believe, however, that he was especially attuned to the Church's doctrines on Sacred Scripture—its truth, authority, inspiration, and inerrancy—which found such robust expression in the council's "Dogmatic Constitution on Divine Revelation," *Dei verbum*.

As many laymen tend to see their wives' best qualities described in the "virtuous woman" of Proverbs 31, so I tend to see St. Josemaría, who is a spiritual father to me, in the words of *Dei verbum*, 25. There, the Council Fathers offer their vision of the ideal priest. As I conclude, I would be so bold as to adapt their words to describe St. Josemaría and so many of the priests who have followed him in Opus Dei and in the Priestly Society of the Holy Cross.

They "hold fast to Sacred Scriptures through diligent sacred reading and careful study."

They take care "so that none of them will become an empty preacher of the word of God outwardly, who is not a listener to it inwardly."

They "share the abundant wealth of the divine word with the faithful committed to them, especially in the sacred liturgy."

They "learn by frequent reading of the divine Scriptures the 'excellent knowledge of Jesus Christ' (Philippians 3:8)."

They "gladly put themselves in touch with the sacred text itself, whether it be through the liturgy, rich in the divine word, or through devotional reading, or through instruction."

And they "remember that prayer should accompany the reading of Sacred Scripture, so that God and man may talk together"; for, in the words of St. Ambrose, "we speak to Him when we pray; we hear Him when we read the divine saying."

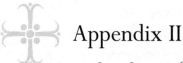

Appendix II

Some Prayers of St. Josemaría

Spiritual Communion

I wish my Lord to receive You with the purity, humility, and devotion with which Your most Holy Mother received You, with the spirit and fervor of the saints.

Prayer to the Holy Spirit

Come, Holy Spirit; enlighten my understanding to know Your commands; strengthen my heart against the wiles of the enemy; inflame my will. . . . I have heard Your voice, and I don't want to harden my heart by resisting, by saying, "Later . . . tomorrow." *Nunc coepi!* Now! Lest there be no tomorrow for me! O Spirit of truth and wisdom, Spirit of understanding and counsel, Spirit of joy and peace! I want what You want, I want it because You want it, I want it as You want it, I want it when You want it.

Prayers for Personal Meditation

Before: My Lord and my God, I firmly believe that You are here, that You see me, that You hear me. I adore You with profound reverence; I ask Your pardon for my sins and the grace to make this time of prayer fruitful. My immaculate mother, St. Joseph, my father and lord, my guardian angel: intercede for me.

After: I thank You, my God, for the good resolutions, affections, and inspirations that You have communicated to me in this time of prayer. I ask Your help to put them into effect. My immaculate mother, St. Joseph, my father and lord, my guardian angel: intercede for me.

Prayer of Acceptance of God's Will

May the most just and most lovable Will of God be done, be fulfilled, be praised and eternally exalted above all things. Amen. Amen.

Prayers to Jesus Christ

Lord, give us Your grace. Open the door to the workshop in Nazareth so that we may learn to contemplate You, together with Your holy Mother Mary and the holy Patriarch St. Joseph, whom I love and revere so dearly, the three of you dedicated to a life of work made holy. Then, Lord, our poor hearts will be enkindled, we shall seek You and find You in our daily work, which You want us to convert into a work of God, a labor of Love.

—FRIENDS OF GOD, 72

With Your help, Lord, I'll fight so as not to be held back. I'll respond faithfully to Your invitations. I won't be afraid of steep climbs, nor of the apparent monotony of my daily work, nor of the thistles and loose stones on the way. I know that I am aided by Your mercy and that, at the end of the road, I will find eternal happiness, full of joy and love forever and ever.

—FRIENDS OF GOD, 131

Lord, I thank You for those tough arms. Thank You for those strong hands. Thank You for that sturdy and tender heart. I was going to thank You also for my errors! No, You don't want them! But You understand them, and excuse them and forgive them.

—FRIENDS OF GOD, 148

Prayers to the Blessed Virgin Mary

Holy Mary, Star of the Sea, Morning Star, help your children. Our zeal for souls must know no frontiers, for no one is excluded from Christ's love. The three kings were the first among the Gentiles to be called. But once the redemption had been accomplished, "there is neither male nor female"—there is no discrimination of any type—"for you are all one in Christ Jesus."

—CHRIST IS PASSING BY, 38

Cor Mariae Dulcissimum, iter para tutum: Most Sweet Heart of Mary, prepare a safe way. Guide our steps on earth with strength and security. Become for us the path we are to follow, since you in your love know the way, a sure shortcut, to the love of Jesus Christ.

—CHRIST IS PASSING BY, 178

Advice on Offering Your Work to God

Turn to Our Lord with confidence and say to Him: "I don't feel like doing this at all, but I will offer it up for You." And then put your heart into the job you are doing, even though you think you are just play-acting. Blessed play-acting! I assure you it isn't hypocrisy, because hypocrites need a public for their pantomimes, whereas the spectators of our play, let me repeat, are the Father, the Son, and the Holy Spirit, the Most Holy Virgin, St. Joseph, and all the Angels and Saints in Heaven.

—FRIENDS OF GOD, 152

Prayer for the Intercession of St. Josemaría

O God, through the mediation of Mary Our Mother, You granted Your priest St. Josemaría countless graces, choosing him as a most faithful instrument to found Opus Dei, a way of sanctification in daily work and in the fulfillment of the Christian's ordinary duties. Grant that I too may learn to turn all the circumstances and events of my life into occasions of loving You and serving the Church, the pope, and all souls with joy and simplicity, lighting up the pathways of this earth with faith and love. Deign to grant me, through the intercession of St. Josemaría, the favor of . . . [make your request]. Amen.

Our Father, Hail Mary, Glory be to the Father.

 # Bibliography

PRIMARY DOCUMENTS

I have cited certain works by St. Josemaría so frequently that I thought it best, in the notes, to refer to them just by title and numbered section. When I cite particular passages, I provide the section number and not the page number; these should be uniform across all editions of St. Josemaría's works.

Here I provide bibliographic details about the editions I consulted. There is nothing special about these particular editions; they are not necessarily the most official, most definitive, or most annotated. They are the editions I happen to have at hand for my prayer. More information about the founder's published works is available online at www.escriva-works.org.

All Church documents are available online at www.vatican.va.

Christ Is Passing By. Manila: Sinag-Tala, 1991.
Conversations with Monsignor Escrivá de Balaguer. Manila: Sinag-Tala, 1985.
The Forge. New York: Scepter, 1988.
Friends of God. Manila: Sinag-Tala, 1991.
Furrow. Manila: Sinag-Tala, 1991.
Holy Rosary. New York: Scepter, 2003.

In Love with the Church. New York: Scepter, 1989.

The Way. Manila: Sinag-Tala, 1991.

Way of the Cross. New York: Scepter, 1987.

 Notes

CHAPTER 1: A PERSONAL PRELUDE

6   "It was not a pastoral project . . ." Missal for the beatification of
    Josemaría Escrivá de Balaguer and Josephine Bakhita (Vatican City:
    Tipografia Vaticana, 1992), 20.

6   "Ordinary Christians. A fermenting mass . . ." "Apuntes intimos"
    (private notes), quoted in José-Luis Illanes, "Work, Justice,
    Charity," in *Holiness and the World,* ed. M. Belda et al. (Princeton,
    N.J.: Scepter, 1997), 211.

7   ". . . in every place in the world . . ." Andrés Vázquez de Prada,
    The Founder of Opus Dei: The Life of Josemaría Escrivá, vol. 1, *The Early
    Years* (Princeton, N.J.: Scepter, 2001), 287.

7   Josemaría Escrivá, letter, March 28, 1955, no. 3, cited in *The
    Canonical Path of Opus Dei,* ed. Fernando Ocariz et al. (Princeton,
    N.J.: Scepter, 1994), 271.

11 For other books on Opus Dei, see, for example, ibid.; Pedro
    Rodríguez et al., *Opus Dei and the Church* (Dublin: Four Courts,
    1994); John L. Allen Jr., *Opus Dei* (New York: Doubleday, 2005).

CHAPTER 2: THE SECRET OF OPUS DEI

14 The story about the young priest is a fixture in the oral tradition of
    Opus Dei. It is told briefly in Peter Berglar, *Opus Dei: Life and Work of
    Its Founder, Josemaría Escrivá* (Princeton, N.J.: Scepter, 1993), 75.

17   "the whole of God Himself" *Difficulty* 41 (1308B), in Andrew
      Louth, *Maximus the Confessor* (London: Routledge, 1996), 158.

18   "was making spring forth in my heart . . ."Vázquez de Prada,
      Founder of Opus Dei, 1:295.

18   "a prayer of copious and ardent feelings of affection." Ibid., 294.

19   "Divine filiation . . . as the basis . . ." *Christ Is Passing By,* 64.

19   "By living their divine filiation . . ."Vázquez de Prada, *Founder of
      Opus Dei,* 1:296.

20   "as old as the Gospel but . . ." *In Love with the Church,* 26.

21   "by his death, Christ liberates us from sin . . ." *Catechism of the
      Catholic Church,* no. 654.

21   In Hebrew, as in Greek and other ancient languages, the same word
      signifies "spirit,""breath," and "wind."

22   See "Is Man to Become God? On the Meaning of the Christian
      Doctrine of Deification," in Christoph Schönborn, *From Death to
      Life:The Christian Journey* (San Francisco: Ignatius, 1995), 41–63.

23–24   "The work of our Redemption . . ." *Way of the Cross,* 14.

24   "A man becomes God . . ." *Christ Is Passing By,* 8.

CHAPTER 3: THE CATHOLIC WORK ETHIC

26   "From the beginning of creation man has had to work . . ." *Friends
      of God,* 57.

28–29   "But the striking way . . ." C. F. D. Moule, *The Birth of the New
      Testament* (San Francisco: Harper & Row, 1981), 43.

29–30   "the temptation . . . to lead a double life . . ." and "No, my
      children!" and "That is why I tell you . . ." are all found in
      "Passionately Loving the World," a homily *In Love with the Church,* 52.

32   "Let us bless pain . . ." *The Way,* 208.

34   "Christ has no body now but yours . . ." is from the adaptation that

John Michael Talbot set to music in "St. Theresa's Prayer," *The John Michael Talbot Collection* (Sparrow, 1995).

CHAPTER 4: THE WORK AND THE CHURCH

38 "as old as the gospel . . ." Rodríguez et al., *Opus Dei and the Church,* 34.

39 "people who set an example . . ." Letter quoted in ibid., 10.

39 "the Church is present wherever . . ." *Conversations with Monsignor Escrivá de Balaguer,* 112.

39 "I hope the time will come . . ." Ibid., 66.

40 "Opus Dei is a little bit of the Church." Quoted in Rodríguez et al., *Opus Dei and the Church,* 1.

40 "The structure of the Church . . . is this . . ." Rodríguez et al., 32.

41 "The prejudice that ordinary members . . ." *Conversations with Monsignor Escrivá de Balaguer,* 21. St. Josemaría is quoting here something he wrote in 1932.

41 The distinction between ordained priests and the lay faithful is not just one of function; it involves a distinct way of participation in the priesthood of Christ. It's not only a question of degree but of essence (cf. Second Vatican Council, *Lumen gentium,* 10).

42 "The idea of priests and laity . . ." Allen, *Opus Dei,* 38.

42 On Jerome's attitudes toward marriage, see his letter (22.20–21) to Eustochium: "I praise wedlock, I praise marriage—but it is because they produce virgins for me."

43 "It is clear that, through our vocation . . ." Quoted in Rodríguez, *Opus Dei and the Church,* 2.

44 "an apostolic organism . . ." Apostolic Constitution *Ut Sit,* Pope John Paul II, November 28, 1982.

44 "The Church's richness . . ." Rodríguez, 37.

44   "A family within the great *familia Dei* . . ." Ibid., 38.

47   "Love for the world and for the Church . . ." Quoted in ibid., x.

CHAPTER 5: WORK AND WORSHIP: THE PLAN OF LIFE

50   "So much is happening so fast . . ." James Watson, address to the
World Economic Forum in 1990, quoted in Richard John Neuhaus,
"The Excitable Dr. Watson," *First Things* (June–July 1990): 67.

53   "put your professional interests in their place . . ." *Furrow*, 502.

53   "I have always seen rest . . ." Ibid., 514.

56   "You must above all stick to your daily periods of prayer . . ." Ibid.,
994.

57   "the most sacred and transcendent act . . ." *In Love with the Church*, 51.

57   "Receiving the Body and Blood of Our Lord . . ." Ibid.

57   "the presence of the Eucharist in a Christian's life . . ." Bishop
Javier Echevarría, "Ordinary Work to Be Offered on the Altar,"
Avvenire (Milan, Italy), October 31, 2005, available in translation at:
www.opusdei.org.

58   "Keep struggling, so that the Holy Sacrifice . . ." *The Forge*, 69.

58   "For their work, prayers, and apostolic endeavors . . ." *Lumen
gentium*, 34.

CHAPTER 6: AIMING HIGH

63–4 For the biblical prohibition against choosing items of lesser value
for sacrifice see, for example, Leviticus 22:20–24.

64   "Those who are 'ambitious' . . ." *Furrow*, 625.

64   "better themselves through human labors." *Lumen gentium*, 41.

65   "should raise all of society . . ." Ibid.

65   "Throughout the course of the centuries . . ." *Gaudium et spes*, 34.

67   "Reject any ambition for honors." *Furrow,* 976.

67   "You tell me . . ." *The Way,* 822.

67–8 "For want of a nail . . ." Benjamin Franklin, "Poor Richard's Almanack," June 1758, in *The Complete Poor Richard Almanacks,* facsimile ed., vol. 2 (Barre, Mass: Imprint Society, 1970), 375, 377. Franklin's aphorism finds a homey echo in St. Josemaría's *The Way* (830), where the founder speaks of each individual believer as a "little bolt in that great undertaking of Christ's."

68   "You have the power to transform . . ." *Friends of God,* 221.

69   "mystical wishful thinking" *In Love with the Church,* 53. The Spanish phrase *mistica ojalatera* is an audible pun that suggests both "if-only mysticism" and "tin-can mysticism."

69   "Do not lose that holy ambition of yours . . ." *Furrow,* 976.

70   "pulled down the visor of his beat-up dusty, old car . . ." Quoted from private correspondence with the author.

71   "Have you seen how that imposing building was built?" *The Way,* 823.

71   "everyone should make legitimate use . . ." *Compendium of the Social Doctrine of the Church,* 336.

71–2 "By means of work . . ." Ibid., 265.

CHAPTER 7: FRIENDSHIP AND CONFIDENCE

76–8 On St. Josemaría looking to these "early Christians" for inspiration and instruction see, for example, *The Way,* 971, and *Friends of God,* 225. For an excellent study of the subject, see "The Example of the Early Christians in Blessed Josemaría's Teachings," *Romana* (bulletin of the Prelature of the Holy Cross and Opus Dei) (July–December 1999): 292–306, available online at www.Romana.org.

76–8 For a detailed sociological analysis of Church growth at this time, see Rodney Stark, *The Rise of Christianity* (San Francisco:

HarperSanFrancisco, 1998). See also the interview with Stark, "A Double-Take on Early Christianity," *Touchstone* (January–February 2000), available online at: www.touchstonemag.com.

77   "Christians are distinguished from others . . ." I have adapted the quotations from the *Letter to Diognetus* from the now rather antiquated translation in the University of Edinburgh's Ante-Nicene Fathers series of the late nineteenth century. The full English translation, as well as the Greek original, can be found at www.ccel.org.

78   "We began just yesterday . . ." Tertullian, *Apology,* 37.4.

78   "Christ known to others . . ." *Lumen gentium,* 31.

78   "apostolate of friendship and confidence." *Conversations with Monsignor Escrivá de Balaguer,* 62, 66.

78–9   David Scott, *A Revolution of Love: The Meaning of Mother Teresa* (Chicago: Loyola, 2005), 61–62.

79   "I'll place a martyrdom within your reach . . ." *The Way,* 848.

79   "Out of a hundred souls . . ." *Furrow,* 183.

81   "sanctifying others through work" See, for example, *Conversations* 10.

81   "first, prayer; then atonement . . ." *The Way,* 82.

81–2   The story about the soccer teams from Spanish jails appears in John F. Coverdale, *Uncommon Faith: The Early Years of Opus Dei, 1928–1943* (Princeton, N.J.: Scepter, 2002), 114.

82   "never failed to point out . . ." The quote and the commentary appear in "Patrimony for the Entire Church," an interview with Javier Echevarría, *Paulina Lo Celso* (Argentina), January 6, 2003.

82   "See how they love one another." Tertullian, *Apology,* 39.1.

CHAPTER 8: SECULARITY AND SECULARISM

86   "Religion cannot be separated from life . . ." *Furrow,* 308.

87   "But where they really meet . . ." *In Love with the Church,* 54.

88   "By reason of their special vocation . . ." *Lumen gentium,* 4; *Catechism of the Catholic Church,* 898.

88   "To permeate and perfect the temporal order . . ." *Code of Canon Law,* 225.

88   "Nothing distinguishes my children . . ." *Conversations with Monsignor Escrivá de Balaguer,* 118.

88–9   On the problem of clericalism, no analysis has been more clear or constructive than that of Russell Shaw. His is a voice crying out in the wilderness. See especially his books *Catholic Laity in the Mission of the Church* (Bethune, S.C.: Requiem, 2005), *To Hunt, to Shoot, to Entertain: Clericalism and the Catholic Laity* (San Francisco: Ignatius, 1993), *Ministry or Apostolate: What Should the Catholic Laity Be Doing?* (Huntington, Ind.: Our Sunday Visitor, 2002), and, with Germain Grisez, *Personal Vocation: God Calls Everyone by Name* (Huntington, Ind.: Our Sunday Visitor, 2003).

90   For further information on how St. Josemaría revered the work of religious orders, see Andrés Vázquez de Prada, *The Founder of Opus Dei: The Life of Josemaría Escrivá,* vol. 2, *God and Daring* (New York: Scepter, 2003), 326. See also "One Hundred Years Down the Little Way," *Our Sunday Visitor,* September 28, 1997.

90   "the death knell of clericalism." Allen, *Opus Dei,* 374.

90   "Live as others around you live . . ." *The Forge,* 508.

91   "The Lord wants his children . . ." Ibid., 703.

92   The question of how it is possible for people to do "good works" even apart from the state of grace was treated very well by Pope John Paul II in his General Audience for November 10, 1993, "Jesus's Earthly Life Is a Model for the Laity," available online at: www.vatican.va.

92   "all the works of nonbelievers . . ." Denzinger-Schönmetzer, n. 1925.

93   "Because human nature is not altogether corrupted . . ." *Summa Theologica,* I–II, q. 109, a. 2.

94   "passionately loving the world" This is the title of St. Josemaría's
      most famous homily, printed in *In Love with the Church* and in
      Conversations with Monsignor Escrivá de Balaguer.

94   "The world awaits us." *Furrow,* 290.

CHAPTER 9: SEX AND SACRIFICE

95   "God in His deepest mystery . . ." Pope John Paul II, *Puebla: A
      Pilgrimage of Faith* (Boston: Daughters of St. Paul, 1979), 86.

95   On the relationship between God and "family," it is crucial to note
      that there are important distinctions to be made between human
      families and the "divine family." See, for example, *Catechism of the
      Catholic Church,* nos. 239, 370.

96   "My son, you wouldn't please God . . ." Transcript from a gathering
      at Tajamar in Madrid, Spain, October 28, 1972. Thanks to Instituto
      Histórico San Josemaría for the material from these and other
      unpublished transcripts.

96   "I speak about the sacrament of matrimony . . ." Transcript from a
      gathering at Guadalaviar in Valencia, Spain, November 18, 1972.

98–9 "On the one hand, there is the joy of knowing . . ." *Christ Is
      Passing By,* 24.

98–9 "I've often said that the hardest mortification . . ." Transcript
      from a gathering at Club Xénon in Lisbon, Portugal, November 3,
      1972.

99   "Love, my children, is sacrifice." Ibid.

99   "shouldn't take their husbands for granted." Ibid.

99   "never lose the refinement you had . . ." Ibid.

99   "make sacrifices cheerfully, inconspicuously." Ibid., November 4,
      1972.

100   "Sex is something noble and holy . . ." *Friends of God,* 185.

100 "Marriage is a sacrament that makes one flesh . . ." *Christ Is Passing By,* 24.

101 "Fear of having children . . ." Transcript from a gathering at Pozoalbero, Jerez de la Frontera, November 12, 1972.

101 "Don't tolerate this infamous, anti-Christian propaganda . . ." Ibid.

102 "God, in His providence . . ." Ibid.

103 "Many live like angels . . ." *The Way,* 122.

CHAPTER 10: THE WORKSHOP OF NAZARETH: ON UNITY OF LIFE

108 "There is only one life . . ." *In Love with the Church,* 52.

109 "Our Lord does not expect us to be unhappy . . ." *Christ Is Passing By,* 126.

110 "This unity of life built on the presence of God . . ." Ibid., 11.

110 "To work in this way is to pray . . ." Ibid., 10.

111 "Jesus does not allow any division here . . ." *Friends of God,* 165.

CHAPTER 11: A WORKING MOTHER

114 "Our mother is a model of correspondence to grace . . ." *Christ Is Passing By,* 173.

APPENDIX I: ST. JOSEMARÍA AND SCRIPTURE

123–24 "This doctrine of Sacred Scripture . . ." *Conversations with Monsignor Escrivá de Balaguer,* 116, 114.

124 "This I have been teaching . . ." Ibid., 52.

124 "When you receive Our Lord in the Holy Eucharist . . ." *The Forge,* 991.

125 "I was myself always impressed . . ." Álvaro del Portillo, *Immersed in*

God: St. Josemaría Escrivá, Founder of Opus Dei, as Seen by His Successor, Bishop Álvaro del Portillo, interview by Cesare Cavalleri (Princeton, N.J.: Scepter, 1996), 121.

125   "as old as the Gospel . . ." *In Love with the Church,* 26.

125   "How I wish your bearing . . ." *The Way,* 2.

125   "They seem not to have read the Gospel." *Furrow,* 26.

126   "In our own life . . ." *Christ Is Passing By,* 14.

126   "gave constant proof . . ." Ibid., 119.

127   "I advised you to read . . ." *Furrow,* 672; see also *Friends of God,* 222.

127   "Make it a habit to mingle . . ." *Friends of God,* 216.

127–28 "For we do need to know it well . . ." *Christ Is Passing By,* 89.

128   "If we do this without holding back . . ." Ibid.

128   "divine filiation is the basis . . ." Ibid., 64.

128   "in an explicit, clear, definitive way . . ." Vázquez de Prada, *Founder of Opus Dei,* 295–96.

129   "the books of both the Old and New Testaments . . ." *Dei verbum,* 11.

130   "One sign of his reverence . . ." Del Portillo, *Immersed in God,* 121.

130   "For the Church has traditionally interpreted . . ." *Catechism of the Catholic Church,* nos. 115–17.

130   "profundity and immediacy . . ." Del Portillo, *Immersed in God,* 121.

131   St. Josemaría used this image of Esau in several places; see, for example, *Friends of God,* no. 13.

131   "All other senses . . ." *Summa Theologica,* I,1,10 ad 1; cf. *Catechism of the Catholic Church,* no. 116.

132   "when I raised the host . . ." Letter of December 29, 1947, quoted in Vázquez de Prada, *Founder of Opus Dei,* 287.

132   "it is above all through the liturgy . . ." Pontifical Biblical Commission, *The Interpretation of the Bible in the Church,* IV.c.1.

133   "always timely witnesses." *Catechism of the Catholic Church,* no. 688.

133 It's worth thinking about . . ." *Christ Is Passing By,* 63.

135 "Like the Fathers of the Second Vatican Council . . ." See, for example, ibid., 116, 118, 122; *The Forge,* no. 437.

135 "You have just been listening . . ." *Conversations with Monsignor Escrivá de Balaguer,* 112.

136 "We now listen to the word . . ." *Christ Is Passing By,* 89.

SCOTT HAHN is a professor of theology and Scripture at the Franciscan University of Steubenville and was recently appointed to the Pope Benedict XVI Chair of Biblical Theology and Liturgical Proclamation of Saint Vincent Seminary (Latrobe, Pennsylvania). He is the author of more than a dozen books, including *The Lamb's Supper*; *Hail, Holy Queen*; *Swear to God*; and *Understanding the Scriptures*. He lives in Steubenville, Ohio.